D0333495

# THE RAF

**The Royal Air Force Ensign**  Sir Hugh Trenchard represented to
King George V in 1920 that many airmen had died or had been maimed
flying under the motif of "three roundels superimposed, red upon white
upon blue" and that it was an appropriate emblem for the fly of a
proposed Royal Air Force Ensign. The Royal Assent was given on 24th
March 1921. Here, a Wessex of the RAF trails the Ensign at the
conclusion of a memorable flying display, given on 5th July 1968 to
2,200 survivors who were founder members of the RAF in 1918.

# THE RAF

*A Pictorial History*

BRUCE ROBERTSON

ROBERT HALE LIMITED
LONDON

© *Bruce Robertson 1978*
© *Line drawings and charts Peter G. Cooksley 1978*
*First published in Great Britain 1978*

ISBN  0  7091  6607  9

Robert Hale Limited
Clerkenwell House
Clerkenwell Green
London EC1R 0HT

Photoset, printed and bound
in Great Britain by
REDWOOD BURN LIMITED
Trowbridge & Esher

# Introduction

The RAF, formed by the amalgamation of two existing air arms at a critical stage of the First World War, had difficulty at first in maintaining a separate identity in time of peace. A saving grace was that of relative economy, proven by air policing as a means of military control in areas of British responsibility – in particular in Iraq. This responsibility, together with the unhappy burden of policing in Palestine, was carried out by Mandate granted by the League of Nations. In India, the RAF took over a large part of the Army's traditional role in patrolling the North-West Frontier to protect the plains of India from plundering by the fierce hill tribes. The RAF was seen to have a purpose, and British air power was extended to the Far East.

At home the limited finance available to the new force was channelled into providing a firm foundation, and such famous training establishments as Cranwell and Halton, basically for air- and ground-training respectively, had status equal to operational groups. At squadron level the officers, rank and file were an élite force and probably the most highly trained air arm in the world. Yet there were shortcomings, and the great achievements of the RAF should not blind one to the fact that, when the war came, operationally the RAF was not necessarily the most efficient air force.

In the same way that the British Army lacked armour, so the RAF lacked armament. While 1650-lb bombs had been used in 1918 by the RAF, a 500-lb bomb was the largest service bomb available in 1939, and one markedly inferior ballistically to its German counterpart. The Luftwaffe had fighters with 20-mm cannon in 1939; while the eight-gun Spitfires and Hurricanes of the RAF sounded magnificent in wartime propaganda – in retrospect, when it is appreciated that those eight guns were set to converge to acquire concentration, the absurdity of using massed small-calibre guns instead of fewer of larger calibre becomes evident. Not that this was the RAF's fault, conditioned as it was to using ammunition held in vast stocks.

Bombers at the outset suffered crippling losses in daylight raids, and at night could not locate their targets with the navigational aids available; yet the Luftwaffe had radio beam guides and pathfinding techniques. At a time when the RAF lost hundreds of aircrew in the sea through lack of a co-ordinated air-sea rescue service, the Luftwaffe had ambulance pick-up floatplanes and a chain of rescue rafts.

For close co-operation with the BEF, the RAF allocated a mere four squadrons of Lysanders. Just over twenty years earlier, when the Army had its own Royal Flying Corps responsible for covering a similar frontage, twenty Army Corps squadrons had been deployed. Moreover these aircraft were able to play their part in staying the great German offensive of 1918 without fighter protection, yet the Lysander, with its much more restricted field of defensive fire was withdrawn to Britain within days of the German offensive of May 1940.

The dedication of the personnel – and aircrew, it should be remembered, were volunteers throughout – gave the Force an unshakable morale in pursuing a war aim that united the whole country. A quick response to each threat, led to rapid development of new equipment and techniques, leading to a vast training organization, backing a complex operational organization at home and overseas.

There were few periods when the Force enjoyed a staid existence. From an expansion peak in 1945, there came another run-down, this time conditioned to an integration of short-term National Servicemen, whose unit service would, in general, be far less than time spent on their training. The Cold War and Korean War caused expansion following contraction, followed in turn by commitments to alliances formed as a result of the Cold War. The Western Union of Britain, France and the Benelux countries in 1947, expanded to the North Atlantic Treaty Organization in 1948, followed by the Central and South-East Asian Treaty Organizations (CENTO and SEATO) involving the RAF in Europe, the Middle East and Far East.

In the late 'sixties, the political decision to withdraw East of Suez, and then the surrender of bases in the Gulf, followed by repeated defence cuts, made planning a nightmare for defence staffs. With changing strengths, a set career structure is impossible, and logistic planning inevitably results in wastages. Much detailed forward planning is negated as political decisions overtake planned policies, and with such emphasis on cuts and economies a cult of management tends to replace leadership.

A prime example of the instability of the times to which the Force is subject has been the steady gathering of Ministry of Defence Headquarters offices in the London area in postwar years to achieve maximum efficiency. With centralization almost complete, it is now deemed expedient to spread them around the provinces and in areas that would be affected by devolution.

Again there are suggestions of merging the Services, and, had the Canadian precedent of a unified service proved satisfactory, this might have been a serious consideration. This is a recurring suggestion, first taken seriously in 1922, resulting in the Mond and Weir report of 1926. Those who appreciate the vastly different role performed by the three Services, know that this is as practicable as the amalgamation of our coastguard, police and fire services.

That the RAF will survive as a dedicated corporate body in spite of the maladministration forced upon it by successive political decisions, will depend on the quality of its staff, particularly in the area which it is the trend to describe as middle management, but can hopefully be ascribed to the middle leadership. Here is the body that plans, for the top leadership to accept or reject their leads, and who will in time take their place. They are backed by an officer- and airman-intake under rigid selection, which shows that the Force still intends to build upon rock, however much it is eroded by influences outside its own sphere.

In this pictorial survey, it is possible only to outline representative aspects of the sixty years of the RAF. Certain milestones had to be recorded; in selecting the various aspects, I have tried to touch upon matters not always appreciated. The basic unit of the RAF since its earliest days is the squadron, yet seemingly no one has set this out in detail before or explained how the organization evolved. At times statistics have been included to show the magnitude of some tasks that may not have been realized or appreciated by those not directly involved.

London 1977                                    BRUCE  ROBERTSON

# Acknowledgements

The author and publishers gratefully acknowledge the following sources of photographs: N. Ainsley; L. Anderton; D. L. Beavis; *Bedfordshire Times*; the late Wing Commander D. G. Beeton, MB ChB, AFRAeS; British Aircraft Corporation; Chaz Bowyer; Charles E. Brown; E. F. Cheesman; Peter G. Cooksley; George A. Cull; Ministry of Defence; Group Captain J. O. S. Denholm, A. E. Ferko; *Flight International*; *Flightlines*; Fox Photos; Roger A. Freeman; Dr Giuseppe Federico Ghergo; P. H. T. Green; J. J. Halley; Imperial War Museum; Philip Jarrett; Brian Lowe; V. Monahan; Philip J. R. Moyes; Ray Punnett; K. M. Robertson Collection; C. E. Sargeant MBE; K. Smy; the late R. R. Soar DSC; Wing Commander L. H. Stewart OBE; Group Captain T. Q. Studd DFC; Wing Commander S. Threadleton; Les Whitehouse, and Vosper Ltd.

# AIR FORCE

ORDER IN COUNCIL FIXING THE DATE FOR THE PURPOSES OF SECTION 3 OF THE AIR FORCE (CONSTITUTION) ACT, 1917 (7 & 8 GEO. 5, C. 51) RELATING TO TRANSFER OF OFFICERS AND MEN TO AIR FORCE.

1918. No. 424.

At the Court at Buckingham Palace, the 22nd day of March, 1918.

PRESENT,

The King's Most Excellent Majesty in Council.

Whereas it is provided by Section 3 of the Air Force (Constitution) Act, 1917, that any officer, warrant officer, petty officer, non-commissioned officer, or man, who, at such date as may be fixed by Order in Council, belongs or is attached to the Royal Naval Air Service, the Royal Flying Corps, or any unit of the naval or military forces engaged in defence against aircraft which is designated by the Admiralty or Army Council for the purpose, may, subject to the approval of the Admiralty or Army Council, be transferred or attached by the Air Council to the Air Force without his consent, but subject to such right of objection as is mentioned in that Section:

Now, therefore, His Majesty is pleased, by and with the advice of His Privy Council, to order, and it is hereby ordered, that the date for the purpose of the enactment herein-before recited shall be the first day of April, 1918.

*Almeric FitzRoy.*

**The Royal Naval Air Service**   The Royal Naval Air Service, which had operated as a naval wing of the Royal Flying Corps, was officially recognized as a purely naval air arm from 1st July 1914. On the outbreak of war on 4th August 1914 it had fifty-two seaplanes, thirty-nine landplanes and seven airships on charge, manned by 128 officers and seven hundred ratings. The service grew rapidly and by 1st April 1918, when amalgamated with the Royal Flying Corps to form the RAF, over three thousand aircraft were in service. The main flying boats of the RNAS were the F2A and similar F3 seen above, designed at Felixstowe (hence the 'F'), and the main floatplane was the Short 184 of which an example is seen flying over Mudros. The RNAS was organized mainly on a station or ship basis, but overseas units were organized on a wing and squadron basis, including squadrons of landplanes giving support to the Army on the Western Front. Naval squadrons, numbered from No 1 upwards, were renumbered by adding 200 to their number on formation of the RAF to avoid confusion with former RFC squadrons.

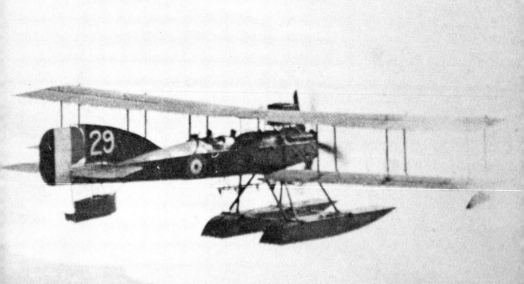

**The Royal Flying Corps**   The Royal Engineers formed an Air
Battalion from 1st April 1911, comprising No 1 (Airship) Company,
South Farnborough, and No 2 (Aeroplane) Company, Larkhill. By
Royal Warrant dated 13th April 1912, this Battalion was integrated on
13th May into a new organization, the Royal Flying Corps, comprising
Military and Naval Wings, a Central Flying School opening at Upavon
on 19th June, a Reserve and the Royal Aircraft Factory. Military trials
of aeroplanes that August established initial standardization on the BE2
series, of which a BE2c is seen above in Mesopotamia *circa* 1916. In
August 1914 the Corps had 147 officers, 1,097 men, 179 aircraft and 320
vehicles. That month four squadrons formed part of the British
Expeditionary Force in France. In November the squadrons were
reorganized into Wings attached to Army Corps, and the RFC expanded
rapidly at home and overseas. In 1913 all airships passed to the RNAS,
but the RAF maintained a large balloon training organization and
deployed five balloon wings, each averaging four companies, in France
alone by 1918. A balloon section is illustrated below.

**Heritage of a Force**   The official date of the amalgamation of the
Royal Naval Air Service and the Royal Flying Corps to form the RAF,
1st April 1918, was essentially an administrative date, putting into effect
a Third Service. But the routine, uniforms, customs and, more
important, operations were little affected for some months. Until the
formation of the RAF, the pilot and observer entry had been mainly by
transfer from other arms of the Army. With the formation of a new

12

service, a large entry from civilian life was necessary, and a Cadet
Brigade was formed to initiate recruits into military life, drill, service
etiquette and, even in this first year of the new Service, a pride in the
achievements of airmen to date, spelt out here by the cadets on parade at
Hastings, 1918. NCOs and men aspiring to commissions were given a
special two-month course.

**The Schools of Aeronautics** The next stage in becoming a pilot or observer was two months' ground instruction at a School of Aeronautics. These were:

No 1 Reading
No 2 Oxford
No 3 Heliopolis
(Middle East entrants)
No 4 Toronto
(Canadian entry)
No 5 Denham
No 6 Bristol
No 7 Bath
(for observers)
No 8 Cheltenham
Nos 9 and 10 planned

Scenes at Schools of Aeronautics. A synthetic trainer of 1918 for spotting instruction using a DH2 nacelle. Subjects taught were theory of flight, rigging, aero-engines, armament, map reading, artillery observation, photography and signalling. Pupils were classed as cadets and on passing out they were gazetted 2nd Lieutenants on probation and posted to a Training Depot Station. Here they are seen at a requisitioned Oxford college.

**Training Depot Stations** By 1918 a vast training organization had been built up, with training squadrons grouped together in threes at Training Depot Stations of which over sixty were operated in the United Kingdom, four in Egypt and two in France at Vendôme. Above is the scene at No 71 TDS at Port Meadow, Oxford, May 1918, with a flight shed, seven canvas Bessoneaux hangars and an RE hangar, and hutted and tented accommodation beyond. The location of these training stations had an important bearing on the disposition of the postwar Force and some of the hangars built at these locations in 1917–18 are still standing. These TDSs were designated by number and located as follows.

| | | | |
|---|---|---|---|
| 1 Stamford (became Wittering) | 17 Abu Sueir | 36 Hylton (renamed Usworth 15.7.18) | 55 Manston (moved to Narborough October 18) |
| 2 West Fenton (re-named Gullane 17.4.18) | 18 Ismailia | 37 Yatesbury | 56–58 Cranwell |
| | 19 El Rimal | 38 Tadcaster | 59 Portholme |
| | 20 Shallufa | 40 Harlaxton | Meadow |
| 3 Lopcombe Corner | 21 Driffield | 41 London Colney | (re-named Scopwick |
| | 22 Gormanston | 42 Hounslow | Oct 18) |
| 4 Hooton Park | 23 Baldonnell | 43 Chattis Hill | 60 Abu Qir |
| 5 Easton-on-Hill | 24 Collinstown | 44 Port Meadow | 61 Tangmere |
| 6 Boscombe Down | 25 Cookstown (re-named Tallaght) | 45 Rendcombe | 201–202 Cranwell |
| 7 Feltwell | 26 Edzell | 46 South Carlton | 204 Eastchurch |
| 8 Netheravon | 27 Crail | 47 Doncaster | 205 Vendôme |
| 9 Shawbury | 28 Bicester | 48 Waddington | 207 Chingford |
| 10 Gosport | 29 Beaulieu | 49 Catterick | 208 East Fortune |
| 11 Old Sarum | 30 Northolt | 50 Eastbourne | 209 Lee-on-Solent |
| 12 Netheravon | 31 Fowlmere | 51 Shotwick | 210 Calshot |
| 13 Ternhill | 32 Montrose | 52 Cramlington | 211 Portholme |
| 14 Lake Down | 33 Witney | 53 Dover (Swingate Downs) | Meadow |
| 15 Hucknall | 34 Scampton | 54 Fairlop | 212 Vendôme |
| 16 Heliopolis | 35 Duxford | | |

**The Gosport System**  The system of training at Training Depot Stations was that propounded by Major R. R. Smith-Barry, known as the Gosport System. It remained the basis of RAF flying training throughout the years. Extracts from Smith-Barry's philosophy of training at Gosport contained these words:

"The chief thing is dual control. . . . The next and most important thing is that dual control is administered after the pupil has gone off alone, as unless a learner has practised doing a given thing, such as turning a good deal, he will not appreciate the details that are shown him. In this way, bad habits are corrected before they have time to get fixed.

"The next thing is that as far as possible advanced pupils have been allowed to fly exactly as they chose, their experiments being limited only by the state of their own nerve. This has not been found to increase casualties. The instructors have been tending always from the passenger's seat, so that the pupil has not had to experience an embarrassing change of seat either just before his first solo or any other time. In this way the instructor has, of course, been deprived of instruments, but I take it that a flyer who could not do without instruments would have less to teach than to learn.

"The object has been not to prevent flyers from getting into difficulties or dangers, but to show them how to get out of them satisfactorily, and having done so, to make them go and repeat the process alone. If the pupil considers this dangerous, let him find some other employment as, whatever risks I ask him to run here, he will have to run a hundred times as much when he gets to France."

Flying training instruction policy which had hitherto been in the province of the Central Flying School, Upavon, now devolved upon Gosport, which became the School of Special Flying, designated No 1 in May 1918 upon the opening of a further school (No 2) at Redcar. It was re-named again in July 1918 as the South-West Area Instructors' School with the opening of instruction schools in Midland, North-West and South-East RAF Areas and in Ireland and Canada.

R. R. Smith-Barry

Avro 504, standard trainer of 1918

Instructors at No 1 Fighting School 1918, left to right: Captains Leacroft, Atkinson, Maxwell, Taylor and Le Gallais in front of a Bristol monoplane, a type not used on the Western Front but which served in Palestine and Salonika.

**Specialist Training**   After TDS a pilot was posted for specialist training. Potential bomber pilots went to a School of Navigation and Bomb Dropping – No 1 Stonehenge (HP 0/400), No 2 Andover, No 3 Helwan (for Egyptian TDS trainees) and No 4 Thetford (light bombers). Army co-operation pilots went to the Artillery and Infantry Co-operation School at Winchester. Potential fighter pilots went to a Fighting School which was re-organized by amalgamating the former RFC Schools of Aerial Fighting and of Aerial Gunnery, the month the RAF was formed. By late 1918 the Fighting Schools were No 1 Turnberry, No 2 Marske, No 3 Sedgeford, No 4 Freiston and No 5 Heliopolis (for Egyptian TDS trainees). An Aerial Fighting School was also established in Canada for the Training Brigade controlling fifteen training squadrons (Nos 78–92) grouped in Wings at Camp Borden, Deseronto and North Toronto.

Gunnery training at No 47 TDS Doncaster, 1918

**The Squadron...**

*Officer Commanding:* Major (pilot, normally not allowed to lead over enemy lines)
*Sections:* Headquarters, 3 Flights 'A', 'B' and 'C', Admin., Armament Stores, Transport.

*HQ:* Officer in charge, Captain or Lieutenant. Personnel one Warrant Officer (Technical), one Flight Sergeant and ten other ranks. Duties: administering and controlling maintenance, cooking and special tasks, eg manufacturing bomb racks, airfield maintenance, incising memorial crosses, etc.

*Flights:* 'A', 'B' and 'C', each commanded by Captain with (fighter squadron) eight pilots (1st or 2nd Lieutenants) for six aircraft plus two reserve. Each flight had a Flight Sergeant and thirty-six other ranks as fitters, riggers, armourers, drivers and batmen, and a blacksmith, sailmaker, coppersmith, storeman, welder, compass swinger and electrician.

*Orderly Room:* Recording Officer (Adjutant) captain or lieutenant, Warrant Officer (disciplinary), Flight Sergeant (clerk), two clerks, telephone operator and motor cyclist. Normally working under or in conjunction with HQ. Duties: to keep records, provide returns as required, administration and discipline of squadron as a whole.

*Armament:* Armament officer, captain or lieutenant, sergeant and five other ranks tasked to maintain all arms, personnel and on aircraft.

*Stores:* Equipment officer, captain or lieutenant, comparable to Army Quartermaster with five other ranks responsible for ordering, issuing and accounting for equipment. Normal establishment of fighter squadron in 1918 was twenty-five aircraft.

*Transport:* Transport Officer, captain or lieutenant and twenty-two other ranks which either operated as a section or was split among flights. Vehicles maintained were two Leyland workshop lorries, six Leyland three-ton tenders, four Crossley light tenders, Crossley touring-car for OC, four P & M motorcycles, some with sidecars, and four trailers.

**. . . the Basic Unit** SE 5A of No 1 Sqn RAF, 1918. With the Sopwith Camel, this fighter was the type most widely used by the RAF. This view demonstrates the main markings of RAF aircraft: the roundel introduced in 1914 and rudder stripes adopted in 1915; the serial number (B8501) allotted to the airframe on production which today continues in the same series and similarly consists of a letter/figure presentation not exceeding five characters; the squadron marking (a circle for No 1 Sqn) allotted by GHQ to squadrons on the Western Front; and the individual aircraft marking allotted by the squadron – letter 'E'.

Standard gun armament of the RAF in 1918 was the Vickers and Lewis gun, both of ·303 calibre. The Vickers gun, fed by a belt of ammunition, was synchronized to fire through the propeller arc and was aimed by the pilot pointing the aircraft by means of an Aldis sight, seen by Lt N. C. Tozer's head in this picture of an RE8 used for Army Co-op work, photography (see camera frame), artillery spotting and ranging. For defence, drum-fed Lewis guns were normally used. Two are seen here yoked in a Scarff gun ring which permitted all-round traverse, high-angle elevation and low-angle depression.

**Organization and Administration**   Each squadron had an authorized establishment as tabled, but strength would vary according to losses sustained. The establishment was the limit to which replacements could be ordered from stores and depots. The monthly wastage rate through operations, fair wear and tear, accident and replacement through obsolescence, was:

| Role | Aircraft types | Per Sqn | Wastage |
|---|---|---|---|
| Fighter | SE5A, Camel, Snipe | 25 | 66% |
| Army Co-op | RE8, AWFK8 | 24 | 50% |
| Fighter Reconnaissance | Bristol Fighter | 18 | 50% |
| Day bomber | DH10 | 12 | —* |
| Day bomber | DH4, DH9 | 18 | $33\frac{1}{3}$% |
| Night bomber | FE2b | 18 | $33\frac{1}{3}$% |
| Night bomber | Handley Page O/400 | 10 | $33\frac{1}{3}$% |
| Night bomber | Handley Page V/1500 | 6 | —* |
| Flying boat | F2A, F3, F5 | 10 | 20% |
| Floatplanes | Short 184 | 18 | 25% |
| Torpedo-carrying | Sopwith Cuckoo | 18 | —* |
| Anti-submarine | DH6, DH4, DH9 | 18 | 25% |

*War ended before type became operational*

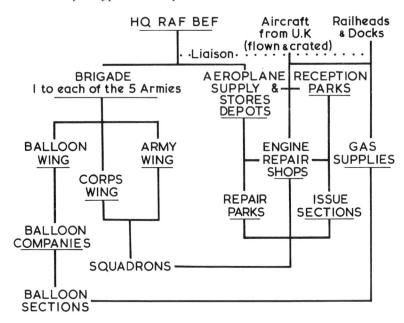

**ADMINISTRATION AND SUPPLY IN THE FIELD 1918**

Workhorse of the RAF in 1918 was the RE8 used by some twenty squadrons on the Western Front in 1918, in other theatres and at home for training. The aircraft had a maximum speed of 102 m.p.h. and an endurance of $4\frac{1}{2}$ hours. This RE8 of No 15 Sqn flew 350 operational hours.

## Action Statistics – 1918

| Theatre | Aircraft destroyed | Aircraft missing | Tons bombs dropped | Photos taken |
|---|---|---|---|---|
| Western Front* | 3,500 | 2,484 | 3,000 | 225,000 |
| Independent Air Force | 150 | 111 | 540 | 3,682 |
| Home Defence | 8 | Nil | Nil | Nil |
| Naval Units | 470 | 114 | 662 | 3,440 |
| Italy | 405 | 44 | 59 | 14,596 |
| Egypt | 25 | 9 | 43 | 8,135 |
| Mesopotamia | 6 | 13 | 25 | 66,720 |
| Salonika | 59 | 8 | 130 | 15,587 |
| Palestine | 81 | 24 | 74 | 27,039 |
| India & Aden | Nil | Nil | 30 | 542 |

* Western Front figures estimated and include about a hundred observation balloons among aircraft shot down. Figures for aircraft missing relate to those lost behind enemy lines. Photographs relate only to plates exposed; prints issued being far greater, eg in October 1918 from 23,247 negatives exposed, 650,000 prints were issued. Specialist RAF photographic staff 1918, was 250 officers and 3,000 men.

An example of the DH9, a standard day-bomber of 1918, that was quickly dropped postwar in favour of the Liberty-engined DH9A.

**Accidents ...** As aircraft increased in size, so the toll rose in crashes. This was one of the worst RAF crashes recorded in the RAF's first year. On a test flight over Maxstoke, fabric was seen to stream back from the lower wing of this Handley Page 0/400 which then nose-dived to earth killing two officers and five air mechanics of No 9 TDS in August 1918.

"They are having bad luck over at London Colney again": so wrote Elliott White Springs in the classic *War Birds – The Diary of an Unknown Aviator* and went on to tell of the Handley Page that nosed down on an Avro and was left on the airfield with its tail in the air – until next day when a Spad taking off crashed into the wreck and knocked the Handley Page on its back.

**. . . and**

**Incidents** Much maligned as the BE2c and DH6 were, they were the safest RAF machines to fly. The figures below show accidents per hundred flying hours and are shown over two months of 1918.

| Type | Aug | Sept |
|---|---|---|
| Avro 504A–K | 1·54 | 2·13 |
| AWFK3/8 | 2·54 | NR |
| BE2c–g | 1·01 | 1·97 |
| Bristol Fighter | 2·26 | 3·11 |
| DH4 | ·95 | 2·82 |
| DH6 | 1·08 | 1·64 |
| DH9 | 4·10 | 2·25 |
| FE2b/d | 1·75 | 2·11 |
| Pup | 3·17 | 3·56 |
| Camel | 6·40 | 5·67 |
| RE8 | 1·81 | 3·81 |
| SE5/SE5A | 2·37 | 5·05 |
| HP 0/400 | ·49 | 2·60 |

Flying hours varied considerably per type, eg 48,885 hours by Avros and 2,526 by SEs in August 1918. Accident causes in one month of 1918:

| | |
|---|---|
| Pilot error or inexperience | 136 |
| Engine failure and forced landing | 61 |
| Collision | 36 |
| Propellers | 28 |
| Design defects | 9 |
| Faulty material or workmanship | 6 |
| Fire or breaking in air | 4 |
| Pilot illness | 3 |
| Weather | 1 |
| Unclassified | 40 |
| Total in one month | 324 |

**A Force on Paper**   The operational part of a force is often called the "sharp end", an apt phrase for the bulk of any fighting force which was, and is, composed of organizers, administrators, supporters, suppliers and transporters. Units with the largest complements were headquarters and depots – for example 1,250 RAF men worked at No 2 Aircraft Depot in France.

A new Force meant new forms and new publications to ensure the smooth-running of the administrative machinery and to increase operational efficiency. Paper was a vital, and the most widely used, method of communication. Here just one week's paper work is reviewed.

In one week of August 1918 the following new or revised Field Service Forms were issued to the RAF by the Air Ministry:

Form 279   Pigeon Log Books
Form 377   WRAF Depot Hostel daily strength return
Form 378   Certificate of Squadron Commanders on charge of command
Form 418   Infectious diseases notification form
Form 428   Daily movements of aeroplane packing cases on charge
Form 434   Nominal roll of officers qualified for full flying pay
Form 437   Report on an officer recommended for staff employment

That same week the following Field Service Publications were issued:

FSP35   Instructions for W/T Transmitter, aircraft, 500-watt quenched spark
FSP36   Characteristics of the ground and landmarks in the enemy lines opposite the British Front from the sea to St Quentin
FSP53   Wavemeter, Heterodyne
FSP54   W/T sets, trench, continuous wave
FSP55   Amplifier Mk IV

Also that week, the Air Ministry issued forty-four orders concerning such diverse subjects as the establishment at Greenwich of a school for flying-pupils suffering from heterophoria; returns of qualified interpreters; free travelling-warrants for other ranks discharged from hospital; dimensions (height, leg inside and arm inside) of officers applying for transfer from aeroplanes to seaplanes; temporary closing of Aldeburgh Aerodrome through structural alterations; price list of Camp Equipment for officers including an improved pattern waterproof canvas bath – 13s. 10d; method of accounting for surgical appliances; land cultivation by RAF Units. One Flying Order was included as follows:

887   Flying Orders – Aeroplanes carrying out Anti-Submarine Patrol Work (B.4234)

In cases where Pilots are compelled to make a forced landing in the sea, they should, if possible, drop their bombs before doing so.

## Equivalent Ranks

| Former rank in Royal Naval Air Service | | Former rank in Royal Flying Corps | | Initial rank in Royal Air Force |
|---|---|---|---|---|
| — | | Major General | | Major General |
| Commodore | | Brigadier | | Brigadier |
| Wing Captain | | Colonel | | Colonel |
| Wing Commander | | Lieutenant-Colonel | | Lieutenant-Colonel |
| Squadron Commander | | Major | | Major |
| Flight Commander | | Captain | | Captain |
| Flight Lieutenant | | Lieutenant | | Lieutenant |
| Flight-Sub-Lieutenant | | 2nd Lieutenant | | 2nd Lieutenant |
| Probationary Flt Sub-Lt | | Officer Cadet | | Cadet |
| Warrant Officer | | — | | — |
| Chief } 1st Grade | | Warrant Officer | | Sergeant-Major 1st Class |
| Petty } 2nd Grade | | Quartermaster Sergeant | | Sergeant-Major 2nd Class |
| Officer } 3rd Grade | | Flight Sergeant | | Flight Sergeant |
| Petty Officer | | Sergeant | | Sergeant |
| Leading Mechanic | | Corporal | | Corporal |
| Air Mechanic | 1st Class | Air } | 1st Class | Leading Aircraftman |
| Air Mech or | 1st Grade | Mechanic } | 2nd Class | Aircraftman 1st Class |
| Aircraftman | 2nd Grade | } | 3rd Class | Aircraftman 2nd Class |
| — | | Boy | | Boy |

The RAF ranks changed as detailed on page 36.

**Qualification for Wearing Wings**   An Air Ministry Order of 8th August 1918 set out the RAF's qualification for the future awarding of Wings and full flying pay (eight shillings a day).

Aeroplane pilots on successfully completing a finishing course at a School of Aerial Fighting, Navigation and Bomb Dropping, Artillery and Infantry Co-operation, Special Training on torpedo-carrying machines; appointment as flying instructor, posting to a mobilizing squadron or an Expeditionary Force squadron or passing tests accorded by 6th Brigade.
Airship Pilots on successfully passing at a finishing school or on posting to a war station.
Observers (single wing) on completing observer's course, on posting to a squadron mobilizing or with the Expeditionary Force, or passing tests set by 6th Brigade.

**The Independent Air Force**    The Independent Air Force, formed on
6th June 1918 under Major General Sir Hugh Trenchard, was the first
force to wage war completely independent of naval or military
considerations. Its ten squadrons of bombers (Handley Page 0/400s,
DH9As, DH9s, DH4s and FE2bs) and one of fighters (Camels) for
escort work attacked industrial and military targets in Germany. The
largest single bomb dropped was of 1,660 lb. As a measure of their
activity, the Force Operations Summary for one month is given opposite.

**Independent Air Force at Peak Strength late 1918**

*Operational Control*
41st Wing (Nos 45, 55, 99, 104, 110 Sqns)
83rd Wing (Nos 97, 100, 115, 215, 216 Sqns)
No 6 Aircraft Park (Repair, Stores and MT Sections)
Nos 5, 10, 12 Reserve Lorry Parks
Nos 11, 14, 21, 27 Tent Detachments
No 3 Aircraft Depot
Nos 8, 11, 12 Air Armament Columns
Port Detachment, Cherbourg

*Administrative Control*
Nos 205 and 212 Training Depot Stations, Vendôme

*Advance Planning*
85th and 88th Wings (RAF Sqns mobilizing in UK)
American Handley Page Sqns with Training Depot Stations at Ford
Junction, Rustington, Southbourne and Tangmere.


The main tool of the Independent Air Force, the Handley Page 0/400.

## —A Strategic Concept

Operations Despatch
August 1918

Hours flown:

| | |
|---|---|
| Day: | 2019 |
| Night: | 846 |

Bombs dropped:

| | |
|---|---|
| 550 lb | 7 |
| 230 lb | 78 |
| 112 lb | 1475 |
| 40 lb | 22 |
| 25 lb | 1105 |
| Cases BI* | 70 |

*(Baby Incendiary)

Weight: $100\frac{3}{4}$ tons

Plates exposed: 704

Hostile machines:

| | |
|---|---|
| Destroyed: | 19 |
| Driven down: | 17 |

Own machines Missing: 27

Own machines Wrecked:

| | |
|---|---|
| DH4: | 16 |
| DH9: | 22 |
| FE: | 5 |
| HP: | 11 |

Ground effect of the IAF (above), a German munitions factory at Qulverain. Below, an FE2b, a fighter reconnaissance aircraft of 1916, that served as an IAF night bomber, remaining in production in 1918.

**War Establishment to Peace Establishment**   The Group is the standard permanent RAF formation, and the squadron the basic unit. Command may vary over the years according to operational expediency by political or area considerations, and intermediate establishments may vary according to a field or station environment.

Instituting an RAF chain of command in 1918 meant imposing a uniform structure on rapidly expanding and complicated service structures. The Army had a dual field (army, army corps, division, brigade, battalion, company) and area (district, garrison, regimental depot, barracks) organization, while the Royal Navy had a fleet and flotilla structure at sea, involving shipboard aircraft, as well as land bases – in particular a chain of aeroplane, floatplane, flying boat and airship stations around coasts at home and in areas overseas.

At home, the former RFC Training Division was disbanded and its TDSs, the Home Defence Brigade and naval stations were placed under Area Command in mid-1918 as follows: No 1 re-named South-Eastern, HQ London; No 2 re-named South-Western, HQ Salisbury; No 3 re-named Midland, HQ Birmingham; No 4 re-named North-Eastern, HQ York; No 5 re-named North-Western, HQ Glasgow.

While units were administered by their appropriate area, the former naval stations of necessity remained under Admiralty operational control. Grouping stations, within an area, according to their function led to the institution of the Group. Each Area was sub-divided into Operational and Training or Technical Groups. The Groups were divided into Wings of two or more squadrons, but several Wings reported direct to areas. Western Front structure was as shown charted earlier.

Before the Command Structure could be streamlined, the Armistice led to a run-down even more rapid than the expansion, and the planning of a peace-time organization for a Service born in war. The Area Command and Group formation structure was retained in a much contracted form. Groups controlled a number of stations, with one to three squadrons each; so that, in effect, a Station equated to a Wing.

The RAF always has more vehicles than aircraft and in late 1918 23,260 were on strength. Until the 1930s, the Leyland three-ton tender (below) was the standard heavy vehicle. All RAF vehicles were finished in khaki until the 'thirties when they were painted blue-grey.

*Numbers of Squadrons Serving – October 1918*

| | | | |
|---|---|---|---|
| Western Front | 84 | India | 2 |
| Independent Force | 10 | Home Defence | 18 |
| Channel (No 5 Group) | 3 | Home Training | 174 |
| Middle East | 13 | Canada Training | 15 |
| Naval | 64 | Egypt Training | 10 |
| Italy | 4 | | 397 |

Plus five Independent Flights on the Western Front and one in Russia.

By early 1922 the structure was

### HOME COMMANDS

*Inland Area*, HQ Uxbridge (Air Vice-Marshal Sir John Salmond) comprising all units in the UK except as below, organized in Nos 1 and 7 Groups and No 11 Wing of four squadrons.

*Coastal Area*, HQ London WC1 (Air Vice-Marshal A. A. Vyvyan) comprising No 10 Group, coastal and experimental stations, carriers and units afloat and recruiting offices.

*Cranwell* and *Halton* each with Area status but commanded at Air Commodore level.

### OVERSEAS COMMANDS

*Middle East*, HQ Cairo (Air Vice-Marshal Sir Edward Ellington) with stations at Aboukir (Aircraft Depot) and Aden (one flight) and controlling Egyptian Group (Heliopolis, Helwan and units at Aboukir) and Palestine Group (Ismailia, Abu Sueir, Moascar, Ramleh and Amman).

*Iraq*, HQ Baghdad City (Air Vice-Marshal A. E. Borton) with stations at Baghdad West, Hinaidi, Mosul, Shaibah and Basrah.

*India*, HQ Ambala (Air Commodore T. I. Webb-Bowen) with stations at Karachi (Depot), Lahore (Aircraft Park) and Nos 1 and 2 Indian Wings controlling six squadrons stationed at Peshawar, Quetta, Kohat, Risalpur and Ambala.

*Mediterranean*, HQ Valletta, Malta (Air Commodore C. R. Samson) with No 267 Sqn at Calafrana, a seaplane base at Feneraki (Constantinople) being dismantled and the carrier HMS *Pegasus*.

The RAF ran three railways in the 'twenties in addition to several special sidings; standard gauge from Birchington to Manston and Sleaford to Cranwell, and narrow gauge from Eaglehurst Camp to the Spit on which the "Calshot Express" is seen below in the early 'twenties. Later the RAF was to operate at peak strength up to 112 locomotives.

## The Russian Expeditions, 1919

An RAF detachment went to north Russia in mid-1918 to prevent Germany's establishing submarine bases in Arctic ports following the signing of the Russo-German peace treaty. In December 1918 they were involved in bombing and strafing for the two British Forces, "Elope" based on Archangel and "Syren" based on Murmansk, co-operating with White Russian Forces. With the Dardanelles open, two squadrons, a training mission and various detachments were sent to south Russia. Following the collapse of the White Russian Forces, all RAF detachments were withdrawing in 1920.

Snapped at midnight in north Russia, summer 1919, left, and Fairey III of RAF Detachment in Bereznik, River Dwina, below.

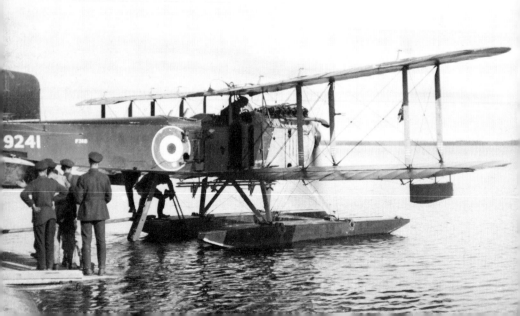

Extract from the *London Gazette*

"His Majesty the King has been pleased to approve the award of the Distinguished Service Order in recognition of gallantry and distinguished service to Flight Lieutenant Walter Fraser Anderson and Observer Officer John Mitchell of 'C' Flight, No 47 Squadron. On July 30, 1919, near Cherni Yar (Volga) these officers were pilot and observer of respectively on a DH9 machine, which descended to 1,000 feet to take oblique photographs of the enemy's positions. A second machine of the same flight was completely disabled by machine-gun fire and forced to land five miles behind the enemy's foremost troops. Parties of hostile cavalry which attempted to capture the pilot and observer were kept away by the observer's Lewis Gun while the pilot burned the machine. Flt Lt Anderson, notwithstanding that his petrol tank had been pierced by a machine-gun bullet, landed alongside the wrecked aeroplane, picked up the pilot and observer and got safely home. . . . The difficult circumstances of the rescue will be fully appreciated when it is remembered that Obs Off Mitchell had to mount the port plane to stop the holes in the petrol tank with his thumbs for a period of fifty minutes flying on the return journey."

DH9A in Russia

Operations over, spit and polish and inspections were part of the life of the squadrons remaining in Belgium and France until the run-down which came after the Armistice terms had been thrashed out at Versailles. Here the men and machines (DH9s) of No 211 Sqn are being inspected by Brigadier General J. F. A. Higgins at Iris Farm, France, late 1918.

**Après la guerre** Gradually the RAF was withdrawn from the Continent. From ninety-seven squadrons and seven independent flights at the time of the Armistice, there were only forty-four in France, Belgium or Germany on 2nd April 1919 when the Army of Occupation was re-named Army of the Rhine. By the end of 1919 only No 12 Sqn was left in the Rhineland, and although the British Army did not leave until 1929, the RAF left in July 1922 when No 12 disbanded.

No 12 Sqn's Bristol Fighters starting up for duty flights with the Army of the Rhine.

**In Occupation**    A Sopwith Camel of No 70 Sqn, which was in the process of re-equipping with Sopwith Snipes, seen at Bickendorf early in 1919. The Camel entering service in 1917 was responsible for the destruction in combat of 1,294 enemy aircraft, more than any other aircraft type.

RAF airfield in Germany. No 12 Sqn's reception area in typical style – Nissen huts, a Tarrant hut, canvas Bessoneaux hangar and the inevitable waiting Crossley tender.

**The First "Airline"**   The RAF's first "airline" was No 1 (Communications) Sqn formed at Hendon, with a detachment at Paris, to provide rapid transport for members of the Government attending the Peace Conference at Versailles. Traffic increases brought expansion to Wing status (the 86th) and Nos 2 and 3 Sqns were formed at Buc and Hounslow, No 4 at Felixstowe, and Nos 5–8 were planned at Bircham Newton. Economy measures forced the Wing to disband in 1920. The RAF's first regular air-mail service was by three squadrons based at Lympne, Marquise and Cologne, for carrying mail between London and the Army of Occupation.

The two aircraft types used by the 86th (Communications Wing), specially fitted Handley Page 0/400s and modified DH4s (below).

**Service Airmail**  The DH10 Amiens (above) was the first regular mail carrier of the RAF operated by No 120 Sqn between Hawkinge and Cologne for the British Army on the Rhine. They were also used on the Cairo-Baghdad military air service which started on 23rd June 1920, and were used in India by No 60 Sqn, whose officers are seen (below) in tropical dress of the overseas dress of the period – khaki drill with Wolseley khaki helmet with khaki puggaree, puttees or field boots.

# Badges and Head-dress

## BADGES OF RANK
### OFFICERS OF AIR RANK

Marshal of the RAF   Air Chief Marshal   Air Marshal   Air Vice–Marshal   Air Commodore

### COMMISSIONED OFFICERS

Group
Captain   Wing
Commander   Squadron
Leader   Flight
Lieutenant   Flying
Officer   Pilot
Officer

### OTHER RANKS

Warrant
Officer   Flight
Sergeant   Sergeant   Corporal   Leading
Aircraftman

### HEAD–DRESS

Air Ranks   Group Captain   Other Officers   Other Ranks

Duty Cap
Officers

Duty Cap
Other
Ranks

Cap Badge
Air Ranks

Officers Full Dress

Cap Badge
Officers

## FLYING AND OTHER BADGES

R A F   Air Gunner
(Pre-1940)   Physical
Training
Instructor   Apprentice   Wireless
Operator   Drum
Major

## ecoming Uniform

n formation on 1st April 1918 the RAF
lopted Army ranks provisionally until
h August 1919 when Air Force ranks as
own opposite were introduced. After the
cond World War, inverted chevrons
ere introduced for technical ranks, but
ith the introduction of a new trade
ructure from 1st April 1964, the inverted
evrons were abolished for reversion to
e traditional badges of rank shown.

he original RAF uniform of light blue
as unpopular, but for a transitional
riod khaki for ex-RFC and blue for ex-
NAS was permitted to the early 'twenties,
y which time the now familiar Air Force
ue had been introduced. Officer styles
e shown from 1922 patterns. Other
nks service and working dress is
ustrated in photographs.

arliamentary Question      4th May 1920
 Captain Wedgewood Benn asked the
cretary for War and Air whether swords
rm part of the uniform of Air Force
ficers and, if so, why?
 Mr Churchill:    A sword forms part of
e full dress uniform of Royal Air Force
ficers. Swords have been worn by officers
the fighting services in this and other
untries, as part of the recognized
signia of their rank.
 Mr Lambert:    May I ask the Right
onourable Gentleman as a great military
nius, whether the sword has not become
obsolete weapon?

*RAF Greatcoat*          *Mess Dress*

*Full Dress*          *Service Dress*

**Policing Policies**    Since 1900 the 'Mad Mullah' had defied military power in Somaliland. But in early 1920 the Mullah was completely overthrown by 'Z' Force made up of DH9As in store, Ford vans and Crossley tenders crated and ferried by the *Ark Royal* to Berbera where equipment is seen (left) being transferred to lighters. The force included a DH9 modified for stretcher carrying which carried out the first operational casualty evacuations.

The RAF deployed few fighters overseas in the early post-war years. The single fighter squadron in India, No 1 with Snipes (type illustrated below), moved to Iraq in April 1921 for convoy protection patrolling and on occasion dispersed armed bands with machine-gun fire. Aircraft operated in their wartime camouflage until 1923 when dope containing powdered aluminium was introduced, both at home and overseas, to give silvery heat-reflecting surfaces to all aircraft except night bombers.

**The Chanak Incident**  When Turkish aspirations, in conjunction with their conflict with Greece, threatened International Treaty areas in the Dardanelles, Britain responded immediately. The *Ark Royal* brought in Nos 4 (Bristol Fighter), 25 (Snipes) and 207 (DH9As) Sqns on 4th October 1922, and No 208 (Bristol Fighters) Sqn arrived from Egypt with a detached flight of Snipes of No 56 Sqn. Fairey IIIDs of No 267 Sqn from Malta and a flight of Nieuport Nightjars of No 203 Sqn from Leuchars were added to the hastily formed Constantinople Wing, plus an Aircraft Park and an Aerodrome Party to develop a site at Kilia while the carriers *Ark Royal*, *Argus* and *Pegasus* stood out in the bay near this location. This view shows the primitive conditions for servicing at Kilia in the early stages of the Turkish sojourn. When the crisis ended in August 1923, the wing was disbanded.

**Foundation in Youth, 1920–25**   Left to right: DH9As, Bristol Fighters, Avro 504Ks and Sopwith Snipes at Halton, 3rd June 1923, represent the lavish allocation of aircraft to No 1 School of Technical Training (Boys) for rigging and engine instruction, as a result of holding wartime stocks. Adult entries in the ranks were trained at the School of Technical Training (Men), Manston, a large station which had its own sidings via Birchington goods station.

Using wartime aircraft, hangars and standby vehicles, as shown in the 1923 Halton scene (below), costs were kept low. But the RAF was planning for the future. In February a Reserve of Officers was formed, and in March the Air Minister, Sir Samuel Hoare, stated that the RAF must be kept a *corps d'élite*, highly trained, well-equipped and capable, so far as possible, of quick expansion. Two months later he was given a Cabinet seat, the first to be held by an Air Minister.

Examinations for RAF Boys, between fifteen and sixteen and a half years, took place twice annually. A limited number had special claims, subject to entry examination, through parental service or circumstances. Successful candidates were attested for ten years' Regular Service, plus two on the Reserve. They received three years' apprenticeship and an education in English, Civics, Practical and Applied Mathematics, Mechanical Drawing and General Science. At successful conclusion of training, they were promoted Leading Aircraftmen or selected for advanced training with cadetships and commissioning a possibility. In the early 'twenties No 1 School of Technical Training (Boys) was divided with part at Cranwell to ease accommodation at Halton, but by the mid-'twenties it was fully centred at Halton. Some idea of the scope of the school can be appreciated by the establishment of officers, alone, commanded by a Group Captain – fifty-eight general duties, ten stores, six accountant branch, and thirty education officers with a university degree normally the minimum qualification.

**Stock in Hand** New aircraft were ordered in small batches, and even these modest orders suffered under the Geddes axe. To replace DH10s on the Cairo-Baghdad air route, an Avro Andover order was cut back to four (J7261–4), the first and last being illustrated. They were retained in the UK for transport and ambulance work from 1924 until the late 'twenties.

In late 1921 all remaining wartime aircraft types had been declared obsolete, except for seven types on which the Force would standardize and for which there were adequate stocks –

| Aircraft Type | With Sqns | With Schools | In Store | Role |
|---|---|---|---|---|
| Avro 504K | 14 | 395 | 514 | Trainer |
| Bristol Fighter | 360 | 227 | 503 | Army Co-op |
| DH9A | 271 | 124 | 268 | Light bomber |
| DH10 | 60 | 7 | 12 | Day bomber |
| F2A and F5 | 45 | 24 | 40 | Coastal patrol |
| Sopwith Snipe | 96 | 39 | 397 | Fighter |
| Vickers Vimy | — | 14 | 71 | Heavy bomber |

Additionally three Vickers Vimy ambulances were retained in squadron use, and thirty-six Vickers Vernon troop carriers were built.

**Post war fighters**    Entering service with Nos 41 and 111 Sqns in 1924,
the Siskin III, developed from a 1918 prototype, represented the first
postwar fighter re-equipment for the RAF. It was also the first service
fighter to be built mainly of metal. The first seventy were followed by the
IIIA which was produced in quantity and differed from the III visually
by the absence of a ventral fin.

Partnering the Siskin, in the postwar fighter squadrons, the Grebe was
the first of a line of Gloster fighters that went into service from 1924. It
was the subject of much experimentation and one became the first RAF
fighter to survive a terminal velocity dive (240 mph). In 1925 service
Grebes were pioneering the general introduction of radio telephony
(R/T) ie speech, to replace wireless telegraphy (W/T) ie Morse Code
signals, used for fighter direction.

**The Iraq Command**    As early as 1919 it was governmental policy to substitute military forces in Mesopotamia (Iraq from September 1921), but the RAF declined until suitable aircraft and trained personnel were provided. Eight squadrons were planned for the task in 1921, of which No 6 Sqn (Bristol Fighters) and Nos 8, 30, 55 and 84 Sqns (DH9As) were deployed. No 1 Sqn (Snipes) was transferred from India, and Nos 45 and 70 bomber transport squadrons of Vernons and Vimys were brought into Iraq Command from Egypt and to maintain a Cairo-Baghdad air mail, as a stage in the development of an air route to India. RAF control in Iraq dated from 1st October 1922 when Air Vice-Marshal Sir John Salmond assumed command.

The Nieuport Nighthawk originally designed to RAF Type 1 Specification issued in 1918, was sent in modified form to No 1 Sqn in Iraq for tropical trials in 1923 but was not adopted for squadron service.

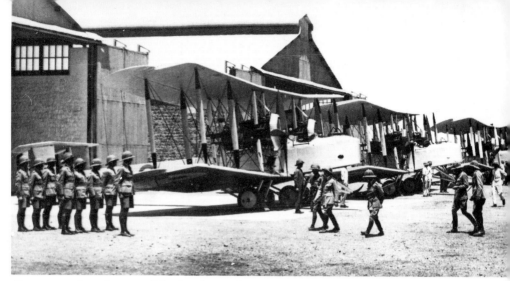

**Overseas Garrisons**   The bugbear of garrison life between the wars was the Air Officer Commanding's inspection, often an annual event. Here, in April 1925, Air Vice-Marshal Sir Oliver Swann, KCB CBE, Air Officer Commanding Middle East, inspects the Vimy Flight at No 4 Flying Training School, Abu Sueir, Egypt. This was the only overseas flying-school of the RAF between the wars.

A continuing RAF presence in Iraq was justified by events. The RAF gave co-operation to ground force columns. In 1925 Sheikh Mahmoud fermented trouble necessitating containing actions. During 1926–7 columns taking punitive action were assisted by the DH9As of Nos 6, 30, 45, 55 and 84 Sqns. Here 'A' Flight of No 30 Sqn are being inspected.

**Station Construction**  Most RAF buildings used after the First World War had been constructed hurriedly during the war and were of a temporary character. Because of stringent economies and a hope that building costs would stabilize, a programme was drawn up of re-conditioning existing accommodation to make it reasonably habitable, pending re-building, which did not come until the mid-'thirties. On the other hand, to provide amenities comparable to the other two services, many married quarters for officers, NCOs and airmen were built in the 'twenties, of sound construction, and are in use today.

There were few amenities at the far-flung outposts of Empire in the Middle East and India. A parody on a song of the period went:

"A little bit of Muttie fell from out the sky one day.
It landed down at Shaibah many thousand miles away,
And when old man Trenchard saw that it looked so grim and bare
He said, 'It's what I'm looking for, to put our Air Force there'."

Electric fans, in spite of electric generating plant at stations, were unheard of in the early 'twenties. A parsimonious Treasury would never have passed them as an amenity. But an essential was a different matter. It depended on good staff work. Explanation of Item 54, Vote 4 of Air Estimates 1923–4 –

"The question of protecting the personnel at stations abroad against the attack of sandfly has been the subject of very careful investigation, as the resultant fever lowers considerably the efficiency of units. As the result of experiment it has been proved that the fly is unable to exist in an atmosphere in which a certain air velocity is maintained. A provisional sum has been inserted in order that work may be commenced on the provision of electrically-driven fans in the sleeping quarters."

Orderly room, No 20 Sqn, Quetta, 1922. Flg Off W. G. Nicholls, acting adjutant, off to tiffin.

**The North-West Frontier**   During 1924 there was much unrest in the North-West Frontier regions of India. In May DH9As of Nos 27 and 60 Sqns and Bristol Fighters of Nos 5 and 28 Sqns took action against the Mahsuds, then in July these squadrons dropped 87 × 230-lb, 68 × 112-lb and 113 × 20-lb bombs, and expended 3,165 rounds of ·303 ammunition in attacks on the Shabi Khel. The wartime aircraft used were wearing out, as anticipated, but since it was taking time to decide on the production of new aircraft types, wartime aircraft such as the DH9A and Bristol Fighter had been put back into production in the early 'twenties. Pictures show a Bristol Fighter serving in India and a No 27 Sqn DH9A after a heavy landing. Both aircraft were built to wartime orders and were shipped to India postwar for service.

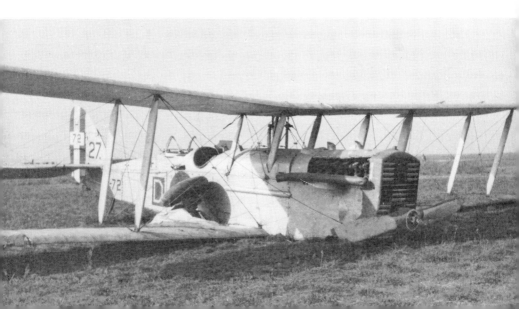

**Proving Parachutes**  Wing-walking, a forbidden antic seen being performed on an Avro 504K of No 4 FTS Abu Sueir (above), was the procedure on Vimy J7441 (below) to get from the cabin to the parachute jumping-off platform on the outer struts, for parachute training.
After much experimentation at Orfordness in 1918, parachutes were adopted initially for Avro 504K trainers in October 1919, and the issue was extended to other aircraft in 1921. The Calthrop Guardian Angle D4 parachute first used in numbers was declared obsolete in 1924 and the RAF standardized on Irving and GQ parachutes.
In 1920 Henlow became the RAF's first parachute centre, and from May 1920 each parachute was numbered and had its own history sheet (Form 329). In 1925 a Parachute Test Centre was established at Henlow and carried out development work, but the basic canopy and harness remained practically unchanged until the advent of the ejector seat after the war. Two basic types of parachute were in use at the beginning of the Second World War, a seat-type for cramped cockpits and a chest-type for crews of larger aeroplanes.

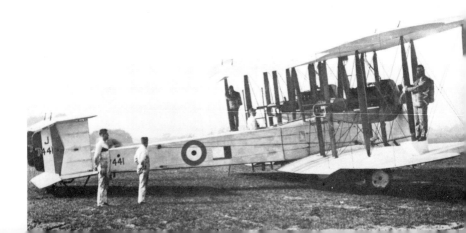

**Proving Flights**  From 1925 the RAF made a series of
long-distance staging flights by formations to assess the feasibility of air
reinforcement and to pioneer Empire air routes. On 27th October 1925
three DH9As under Sqn Ldr A. Coningham started the first of several
Cairo to Kano flights. Wg Cdr C. W. H. Pulford led a flight of four
Fairey IIIDs shipped out from Britain, on the first Cairo to Cape flight.
On return to Cairo, they were fitted with floats and flown to Lee-on-
Solent so completing a fourteen-thousand-mile course. Fairey IIIDs of
the first Cape-Cairo flight are illustrated, one as a landplane and S1102
as a floatplane. The IIID, used mainly by the Fleet Air Arm, equipped No
202 Sqn at Malta and was soon replaced by the improved IIIF. The IIID
version was declared obsolete in March 1933.

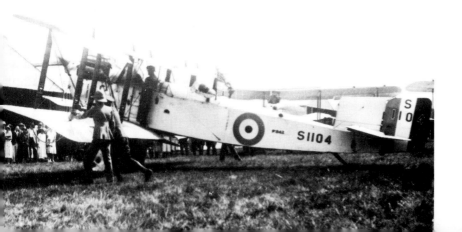

## Strength as at January 1925

| No | Equipment | Station | No | Equipment | Station |
|---|---|---|---|---|---|
| 1F | Snipe | Hinaidi | 28AC | BF | Peshawar |
| 2AC | BF | Manston | 29F | Snipe | Duxford |
| 3F | Snipe | Upavon | 30A | DH9A | Hinaidi |
| 4AC | BF | Farnborough | 31AC | BF | Ambala |
| 5AC | BF | Dardoni | 32F | Grebe | Kenley |
| 6AC | BF | Mosul | 39B | DH9A | Spittlegate |
| 7B | Virginia | Bircham Newton | 41F | Siskin | Northolt |
| 8B | DH9A | Hinaidi | 45BT | Vernon | Hinaidi |
| 9B | Vimy | Manston | 47B | DH9A | Helwan |
| 11B | Fawn | Netheravon | 55B | DH9A | Hinaidi |
| 12B | Fawn | Andover | 56F | Grebe | Biggin Hill |
| 13AC | BF | Andover | 58B | Vimy | Worthy Down |
| 14B | BF | Ramleh | 60B | DH9A | Risalpur* |
| 15B | DH9A | Martlesham Heath | 70BT | Vernon | Hinaidi |
| 16AC | BF | Old Sarum | 84B | DH9A | Shaibah |
| 17F | Snipe | Hawkinge | 99B | Aldershot | Bircham Newton |
| 19F | Snipe | Duxford | 100B | Fawn | Spittlegate |
| 20AC | BF | Quetta | 111F | Siskin | Duxford |
| 22B | (Various) | Martlesham Heath | 207B | DH9A | Eastchurch |
| 24 (Comm) | Avro 504, BF, DH9A | Kenley | 208AC | BF | Moascar* |
| | | | 216B | Vimy | Heliopolis |
| 25F | Grebe | Hawkinge | Note BR = Bristol Fighter | | |
| 27B | DH9A | Risalpur* | * Detachments at other stations. | | |

Four Flying Training Schools were in operation – No 1 Netheravon, No 2 Digby, No 4 Abu Sueir and No 5 Sealand, and there was a School of Army and Naval Co-operation. The standard primary trainer at this time was still the Avro 504K. Over 75% of the aircraft were of World War I design, although many of these were built postwar.

Bristol Fighters (left) of No 5 Squadron in India in the 'twenties.

DH9A (above) being salvaged after a rough landing at a station in India.

## The RAF between the World Wars

*RAF and National Aspirations – First Peace-time Action*

The RAF's first call for military action in civil disturbances in peace-time has had little publicity and even less documentation, for without doubt it was, in jargon of the time, a ragtime affair. Egypt was considered the keystone of the RAF overseas, being centrally placed between Malta and the Middle East and an important staging post. In 1919 No 58 Sqn of Handley Page 0/400 bombers was ordered to move from France to Egypt by air followed by Handley Pages and Vimys of Nos 214 and 216 Sqns, via Paris, Lyons, Marseilles, Pisa, Rome, Foggia, Taranto, Valona, Crete, Sollum and Amria. At the same time No 206 Sqn (DH9s) and No 80 Sqn (Snipes) were sent by sea.

Before these aircraft arrived, the nationalist movement in Egypt had already led to widespread riots, and immediate action was necessary. In the absence of any service squadrons, pilots and observers were formed into 'X', 'Y' and 'Z' Squadrons at Heliopolis and told to select aircraft from a mass of Avro 504Ks left in hangars from wartime training. With these they patrolled railways as an anti-sabotage measure, and on at least one occasion broke up a riot by diving low over demonstrators. The reinforcements arrived in the summer, but some twenty Handley Pages and Vimys were left wrecked or damaged across Europe in the move. Twin-engined bombers, apart from bomber transports, were withdrawn from the area, and ferry flights from Europe were suspended until 1936.

Avro 504K of No 4 Flying Training School, Abu Sueir, *circa* 1925.

## Signs of the Times

### Milking the Ministry!

*From Report of the Comptroller and Auditor General for year ending 31st March 1922.*

"In the course of a local audit at Cranwell by my officers on 1st July, it was noticed that some three hundred out of the 2,500 acres of Ministry property were occupied as a dairy farm. As no receipts for the rent of the farm could be traced, I made enquiries and invited explanation.

"I have learned that farming operations were started by the Admiralty before 1st April 1918 and have been continued since by the Air Ministry with a view to providing milk as required by the station. The position of this undertaking seems to have been so anomalous that I have felt it my duty to bring the matter to the attention of the Treasury, and their Lordships have requested that they may be furnished with the Air Council's observations in regard to it."

### Rabies and the RAF

*Extract from Air Ministry Weekly Order 880 of 14th October 1920*

880 – Danger of Rabies, or Dog Madness

During the past two years some 264 cases of rabies, or dog madness, have occurred in this country. After sixteen years entire freedom of the British Isles from this disease, it was re-introduced into Devonshire by some dogs smuggled from abroad in 1918. The only way to prevent further outbreaks is that all ranks returning from abroad will help the authorities in preventing the entry of dogs into this country unless importation is carried out openly and with proper licence.

Officers and airmen are forbidden to carry dogs by air, whether over the British Isles or elsewhere.

### RAF and the IRA

Early on 1st June 1920 the old Warrant Officers' Mess Room at RAF Cranwell burned out. On the evening of the 4th a large shed reputed to be storing a hundred aircraft was burned to the ground. On 2nd July a large shed containing aeroplanes was also set afire. The damage caused by this series of fires, officially attributed to acts of incendiarism, was estimated at £119,567 2s. 1d. This was a time when IRA activity was rife throughout the United Kingdom, with particular violence in Ireland, leading up to the establishment of the Irish Free State (Eire) in 1922.

### First of the Major Airlifts

The first major airlift was a casualty evacuation of two hundred dysentery cases, by Vickers Vernons to hospital in Baghdad in late 1922 from a column returning from a punitive expedition.

**RAF Life, mid-'Twenties**
*Marriage Allowance – Rates*
1. With reference to The King's Regulations and Air Council Instructions para 3289 the index figure for the cost of living for 1st June 1925 as published by the Ministry of Labour is eighty.
2. Marriage allowance for the year commencing 2nd April 1925 will therefore remain as for the last year at the following rates:

|  | Weekly rate | s | d |
|---|---|---|---|
| For a wife |  | 7 | 0 |
| For a wife and 1 child |  | 13 | 6 |
| For a wife and 2 children |  | 18 | 0 |
| For a wife and 3 children |  | 20 | 0 |
| For a wife and 4 children |  | 22 | 0 |
| For a wife and 5 children |  | 23 | 0 |
| For a wife and 6 children |  | 25 | 0 |
| For a wife and 7 children |  | 26 | 0 |
| and for each other child |  | 1 | 0 |

Air Ministry Weekly Order 94 of 1925, reflects an age before inflation, social security – and the pill!

*RAF and a Stable Economy for a Staple Diet*
From an RAF Order of 1936 – for rations in lieu the following prices and values will be used for the month of October 1936.

| Rations in lieu | Pence per lb | Rations in lieu | Pence per lb |
|---|---|---|---|
| Bread | 1·1 | Meat, preserved | 6·57 |
| Flour | 1·47 | Tea | 15·07 |
| Biscuits | 4·23 | Sugar | 1·87 |
| Beef, frozen | 3·5 | Salt | ·21 |

*RAF and an Unstable Economy*
From Air Ministry Weekly Order 586/23
1  *Official rates of exchange have been fixed as follows:*
    (i)  For the period 20th to 26th September 1923
            German Currency, 6,500,000 marks  . . . . . . . . . . . . . 1d

*RAF and TV*
From RAF Intelligence Summary, November 1938: Television Broadcast of Aircraft
    On 19th October the British Broadcasting Co-operation [*sic*] included in their normal television programme a television broadcast of Nos 56(F) and 151 (F) Squadrons carrying out formation flying at North Weald.

**DH9A, the Workhorse**    Iraq was no easy mandate. Tribal pressures led to the formation of 'Akforce' in November 1928 composed of Nos 55 and 84 Sqns of DH9As and an Armoured Car Detachment, supported by a flight of No 70 Sqn's Victorias which had replaced the earlier Vernons. Detachments supported another column 'Supcol' in the south. One aircraft was brought down by tribesmen. In 1929 an RAF wireless operator was killed by return fire, and the following year Sheikh Mahmoud again caused trouble in South Kurdistan. In all these operations the DH9A was the mainstay bombing, strafing and army co-operation aircraft. Pictured is the Commanding Officer's DH9A of No 55 Sqn in 1928, and F2042, aircraft '3' of 'C' Flight as its markings indicate.

**Armoured Cars**   No 1 Armoured Car Company RAF formed at Heliopolis 19th December 1921 for support operations in Iraq and No 2 formed 7th August 1922 for operations in Transjordan. No 1 later disbanded and its section of Lancia armoured cars were added to No 2 Company operating three Rolls-Royce Sections, two in Iraq and one in Amman. In 1927 armoured cars in Iraq were grouped together as No 1 Wing, reconstituted as a Company on reductions in 1930. Two Rolls-Royce are seen in their sheds, above.

HMAC *Orion*, a Rolls-Royce armoured car with the usual machine-gun armament of an aircraft, a Vickers (in turret) and Lewis (mounted at rear).

**RAF Armoured Car units at Peak Strength, 1925**
No 2 Coy, Sarafand
No 3 Coy, Basrah
No 4 Coy, Hinaidi
No 5 Coy, Mosul
No 6 Coy, Hinaidi

**Army Co-op, Bombing and Fighting. . . .** Army co-operation before radio. A message from ground troops, slung between poles, was hooked by a swooping Bristol Fighter, standard army co-op aircraft of the 'twenties, and retrieved by the gunner. Air to ground messages were placed in weighted canvas bags with streamers attached to draw attention, and were thrown by the gunner.

The twin-engined Sidestrand was the first Boulton Paul product to enter squadron service, and was restricted to No 101 Sqn which used this day bomber for seven years from April 1928. J9179, the fourth Sidestrand built, depicted.

Gamecocks of No 23 Sqn, Henlow, 1926. This Gloster fighter, successor to the Grebe, equipped Nos 3, 17, 23, 32 and 43 Sqns. Normal fighter squadron establishment was three flights of three aircraft plus three immediate reserve plus three stored reserve – and the three furthest from the camera are without engines! The Gamecock was declared obsolete in March 1933.

**The Auxiliary Air Force, 1925–39**    To supplement the RAF in an emergency, additional squadrons were raised on a cadre basis of one or two flights which, in the event of hostilities, could be brought up to strength from the Reserve of Air Force Officers which had been formed from 9th February 1923. Five squadrons, Nos 500–504, were raised with Regular and Special Reserve Officers; but in 1936–7 these squadrons were incorporated in the Auxiliary Air Force (AAF).

The AAF was authorized by an Order in Council of 9th October 1924 under which squadrons were raised on a territorial basis, as listed on page 60. When war was declared, the Force was embodied into the RAF, and the personnel, particularly aircrew, dwindled through casualties and postings as the war progressed as there was no AAF wartime intake. The squadrons then became manned mainly by Volunteer Reserve personnel.

An RAF Guard of Honour presents arms while Group Captain HRH The Prince of Wales turns the key to open the Town HQ of No 601 (County of London) Sqn Auxiliary Air Force at 54 Kensington Park Road, London W11, 21st June 1927.

| Esher Trophy | |
|---|---|
| **Sqn** | **Year** |
| 601 | 1926 |
| 605 | 1927 |
| 601 | 1928 |
| 605 | 1930–1 |
| 604 | 1932 |
| 605 | 1933–5 |
| 604 | 1936–7 |
| 603 | 1938 |
| 604 | 1948–9 |
| 603 | 1950 |
| 616 | 1951 |
| 610 | 1952 |
| 615 | 1953 |
| 609 | 1954 |
| 500 | 1955 |

Marshal of the RAF Sir Hugh Trenchard presents the Esher Trophy for 1929 to No 602 (City of Glasgow) Sqn in the Glasgow City Chambers, seen being received by the Commanding Officer, Sqn Ldr John Fullerton. The Trophy (a statuette of Perseus) was presented annually to the most efficient all-round auxiliary squadron. Other winners and the year are given above.

Most of the Auxiliary Air Forces squadrons proudly displayed their unit number, as did this Wallace of No 504 Sqn.

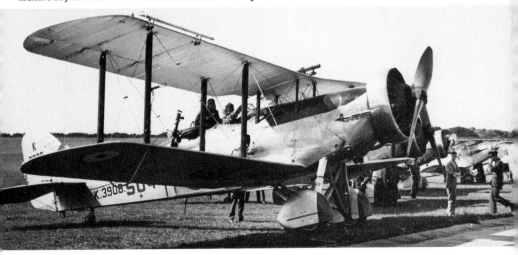

## Auxiliary Squadrons, 1925–39

| Sqn No | Title | Date formed | Station | Aircraft Types Operated |
|---|---|---|---|---|
| 500 | County of Kent | 16 Mar 1931 | Manston and Detling | Virginia, Hart, Hind, Tutor, Anson |
| 501 | County of Gloucester | 14 Jan 1929 | Filton | DH9A, Wapiti, Wallace, Hart, Hind, Hurricane |
| 502 | Ulster | 15 May 1925 | Aldergrove | Vimy, Hyderabad, Virginia, Wallace, Hind, Anson |
| 503* | County of Lincoln | 5 Oct 1926 | Waddington | Fawn, Hyderabad, Hinaidi, Wallace, Hart, Hind, Anson |
| 504 | County of Nottingham | 26 Mar 1928 | Hucknall | Horsley, Wallace, Hind, Gauntlet, Hurricane |
| 600 | County of London | 14 Oct 1925 | Northolt and Hendon | DH9A, Wapiti, Hart, Demon, Blenheim |
| 601 | County of London | 14 Oct 1925 | Northolt and Hendon | DH9A, Wapiti, Hart, Demon, Gauntlet, Blenheim |
| 602 | City of Glasgow | 15 Sep 1925 | Renfrew & Abbotsinch | DH9A, Fawn, Wapiti, Hart, Hind, Gladiator, Spitfire |
| 603 | City of Edinburgh | 14 Oct 1925 | Turnhouse | DH9A, Wapiti, Hart, Hind, Gladiator, Spitfire |
| 604 | County of Middlesex | 17 Mar 1930 | Hendon | DH9A, Wapiti, Demon, Blenheim |
| 605 | County of Warwick | 15 Oct 1926 | Castle Bromwich | DH9A, Wapiti, Hart, Gladiator, Hurricane |
| 607 | County of Durham | 17 Mar 1930 | Usworth | Wapiti, Demon, Gladiator |
| 608 | North Riding | 17 Mar 1930 | Thornaby | Hart, Hind, Demon, Anson |
| 609 | West Riding | 10 Feb 1936 | Yeadon | Hart, Hind, Spitfire |
| 610 | County of Chester | 10 Feb 1936 | Hooton Park | Hart, Hind, Hurricane |
| 611 | West Lancashire | 10 Feb 1936 | Hendon and Speke | Hart, Hind, Spitfire |
| 612 | County of Aberdeen | 1 Jun 1937 | Dyce | Hector, Anson |
| 613 | City of Manchester | 1 Mar 1939 | Ringway | Hector, Lysander |
| 614 | County of Glamorgan | 1 Jun 1937 | Cardiff | Hind, Audax, Hector, Lysander |
| 615 | County of Surrey | 1 Jan 1937 | Kenley | Hector, Gauntlet, Gladiator I & II |
| 616* | South Yorkshire | 1 Nov 1938 | Doncaster & Finningley | Hind, Gauntlet |

* 503 Sqn became 616 Sqn, 1st November 1938

**University Air Squadrons, 1925–39**   There were three University Squadrons pre-war. Cambridge and Oxford formed on 1st and 11th October 1925 respectively, and London in 1935, using RAF stations Duxford, Abingdon and Hendon respectively. In effect they were government sponsored flying clubs, for the pupils had no military obligation; membership was limited initially to twenty-five per squadron, later increased by steps to a hundred. A Wing Commander, chief instructor, commanded, and a small cadre maintained the aircraft. The first two squadrons progressed from Avro 504Ns to Bristol Fighters and then Atlases, but in the 'thirties the Avro Tutor became standard.

Flying instruction was given in term time, and in the long vacation squadrons went into camp at a Service airfield for six weeks with three different courses attended by pupils for two weeks each.

The Bristol Fighters used by Oxford University Air Squadron in the 'twenties are seen above, and their Avro Tutors of the 'thirties below.

**Along the Nile and in Open Waters**   The first RAF operations in the Sudan were by a hastily raised contingent known as 'H' Force for co-operation with a punitive expedition against tribes in south-western Sudan on the Abyssinian border. After four weeks' bombing and machine-gunning, the native chiefs sued for peace, but there were subsequent forays. To co-operate with the Sudan Defence Force, No 47 Sqn was stationed at Khartoum (part of town at top right) from 1927 to 1940, first with DH9As, which in the late 'twenties were replaced by Fairey IIIFs, at first Mk I/IIs (shown) which were made obsolete by the RAF in March 1933. An aircraft also used by the Fleet Air Arm, the Faireys could be fitted with floats as required for operation from the waters of the Nile.

The RAF's one and only flying boat floating dock, used 1922 to 1948, here seen accommodating Supermarine Southampton S1422, a type used by Nos 201, 204 and 210 Sqns at home, No 203 at Basra, and No 205 at Singapore from 1925. Moored in the vicinity of flying boat operations, the dock is shown with wind sock flying.

The first RAF flying boat cruise to the Far East was by four Southampton flying boats which left Plymouth on 17th October 1927 and visited Egypt, India, Hong Kong, Japan and Australia. The aircraft became No 205 Squadron at Seletar, Singapore on 10th December 1928, where they took up station; one is seen operating from the Johore Straits.

**Bombs and Bombers**   The bombs available between the wars, based on the bombs of the First World War exhibited below, left to right: 1650-lb, the heaviest bomb used operationally in 1918; three bombs in the 550/500-lb and three in the 250/230-lb range (one flat-headed for use at sea); 112-lb, 50-lb, 20-lb Cooper and, barely discernible in its white finish, a practice bomb. A 1700-lb bomb was available in 1919 but this, and the 1650-lb bombs, were not used post-World War I. Bomb classifications are misnomers for a 500-lb bomb weighed 700-lb and a 20-lb bomb weighed 32-lb. They were produced in four main types: General Purpose (50–500-lb range), High Explosive (20–550-lb range), Semi-Armour Piercing (250 and 500-lb) and Incendiary (4 and 25-lb). With the exception of incendiary bombs, each bomb was separately cased for transit and a standard three-ton Leyland lorry could, for example, convey 6 × 550-lb or 180 × 20-lb bombs. Bomb loads varied according to aircraft types, but 2 × 550-lb was the maximum load in the 'twenties, and these were rarely exceeded per aircraft in punitive operations between the wars. Supply dropping apparatus was in 28- to 37-lb packs, with different type containers for temperate and tropical use. Main supplies consisted of ammunition, food and water. While the bombs were adequate for their peacetime tasks, the fact has to be faced that ballistically the bombs were inefficient, and Britain lagged behind Germany in this respect in the 'thirties.

The RAF throughout has clung to the policy, originating in the Independent Air Force concept, of a strategic force and that the best form of defence is attack. This was reflected in a revised Command Structure in the mid-'twenties; On 1st January 1925 Air Defence Great Britain was formed under Air Marshal Sir John Salmond; this comprised all units of the Home Defence Force organized under three subordinate commands – Wessex Bombing Area of regular bomber squadrons,

Fighting Area of regular fighter squadrons and No 24 (Communications) Sqn and No 1 Air Defence Group of auxiliary bomber squadrons. All other units, except Cranwell and Halton, which remained independent commands, were under Inland and Coastal Areas. Inland Area controlled the Depots and two Groups – No 22 comprising the Schools of Army Co-operation and Photography, and army co-operation squadrons, and No 23 Group comprising Nos 1, 2 and 5 Flying Training Schools, the Central Flying School and Armament and Gunnery, Technical Training and Electrical and Wireless Schools. Additionally Inland Area administered units functionally controlled by the Air Ministry, such as the Aeroplane and Armament Experimental Establishment, formed at Martlesham Heath on 20th March 1924, and which functions today at Boscombe Down. Coastal Area comprised coastal stations, flights embarked in carriers and all recruiting depots.

Overseas commands remained unchanged, but an RAF China was constituted at Kai Tak, and RAF China on 11th April 1927. That year No 4 (Army Co-op) Sqn was sent to Shanghai to reinforce the Shanghai Defence Force. But apart from the Far East, overseas squadrons had bombing or general purpose roles.

The night bombers between the wars differed in finish from all other aircraft; they were in Nivo, a dark olive green overall, with a red and blue roundel only, so that white did not compromise the camouflage. The aircraft below shown in Nivo is a Handley Page Hyderabad J9296 of No 7 Sqn. Hyderabads replaced the Aldershots in No 99 Sqn in April 1926 and equipped Nos 10, 502 and 503 Sqns, until August 1934, by which time the improved Hinaidi, with Bristol Jupiter radial engines replacing the Napier Lion in-line engines, had entered service in Nos 10 and 99 Sqns. In turn the Hinaidi became obsolete in early 1937.

**Wapiti and Crossley**  J9592, seen flying near the famous Arch of Ctesiphon, was one of many Wapitis despatched to Iraq from the RAF's Packing Depot, Sealand. Arriving at Hinaidi in September 1929 for No 55 Sqn, it was used in operations against Sheikh Mahmoud who had crossed from Persia into Iraq. In 1932 came the Barzan operations involving air strikes against rebel tribesmen, followed by an Assyrian revolt. One Wapiti of the squadron, K1124, was shot down on 8th May 1935 by ground fire over the Middle Euphrates area during a tribal uprising. By this time J9592 had been modified for passenger carrying by the removal of its rear cockpit gun-ring; it was scrapped in March 1937 after flying 1,161 hours.

Below: a ground view of the Arch from the RAF's standard light transport, the Crossley tender. A replacement programme by a series of Morris trucks and tenders took effect in the 'thirties.

**The Airlift from Kabul**    On 5th December 1928, due to the deteriorating situation in Afghanistan and the road from Kabul, the capital, to Peshawar in India being blocked by Afghan Mohmands, it became necessary to evacuate women and children from the British Legation and other nationalities from the city.

Immediately available on the North-West Frontier were twenty-four two-seat DH9As of Nos 27 and 60 Sqns at Kohat, two new Westland Wapitis and a Victoria transport at Quetta. Additionally aircraft from Iraq, 2,800 miles away, were called in. As the Victorias of No 70 Sqn left Hinaidi in pairs for India, so the Victorias of No 216 Sqn in Egypt left Heliopolis to replace them. Additionally, a single Handley Page Hinaidi bomber, on tropical trials in Iraq, moved to India.

A DH9A reconnoitring Kabul on 18th December was shot down by rifle hits in the radiator and fuel pump. Fortunately Flg Off Trusk and LAC Donaldson landed unhurt. Other machines established contact, and when King Amanulla had driven rebels from the city environs, evacuation proceeded from nearby Sherpur airstrip. Initially, Victorias carried women and children, DH9As took baggage and a Wapiti provided wireless contact.

On Boxing Day a German woman evacuee was struck by a propeller and seriously injured; the DH9A concerned had its propeller shattered. The woman survived and was evacuated later; the propeller was replaced by that from Trusk's forced-landed DH9A. Next day falls of snow and poor visibility halted operations for several days, but at the end of December the evacuation of the women and children was complete, and the final flights were made on 25th February 1929 after 268 men, 153 women and 165 children had been airlifted from Kabul to India with 24,193 lb of baggage. Victoria J7926 was abandoned in a forced landing, and a Bristol Fighter was damaged effecting a rescue, plus three DH9As which collected bullet holes; but there were no serious casualties. The picture shows a Kabul evacuation reception scene at Risalpur.

## Strength as at January 1930

| Sqn | Equipment | Station | Sqn | Equipment | Station |
|---|---|---|---|---|---|
| 1F | Siskin | Tangmere | 36TB | Horsley | Donibristle |
| 2AC | BF | Manston | 39B | Wapiti | Risalpur |
| 3F | Bulldog | Upavon | 41F | Siskin | Northolt |
| 4AC | Atlas | Farnborough | 43F | Siskin | Tangmere |
| 5AC | BF | Quetta | 45B | Fairey IIIF | Helwan |
| 6AC | BF | Ismailia | 47B | Fairey IIIF | Khormaksar |
| 7B | Virginia | Worthy Down | 54F | (reforming | at Hornchurch) |
| 8B | Fairey IIIF | Khormaksar | 55B | DH9A | Hinaidi |
| 9B | Virginia | Manston | 56F | Siskin | North Weald |
| 10B | Hyderabad | Upper Heyford | 58B | Virginia | Worthy Down |
| 11B | Wapiti | Risalpur | 60B | DH9A | Kohat |
| 12B | Fox | Andover | 70B | Victoria | Hinaidi |
| 13AC | Atlas | Netheravon | 84B | Wapiti | Shaibah |
| 14B | DH9A | Amman | 99B | Hinaidi | Upper Heyford |
| 15 | (various) | Martlesham | 100B | Horsley | Bicester |
| 16AC | BF | Old Sarum | 101B | Sidestrand | Andover |
| 17F | BF | Upavon | 111F | Siskin | Hornchurch |
| 19F | Siskin | Duxford | 202 (FB) | Fairey IIID | Malta |
| 20AC | BF | Peshawar | 203 (FB) | South-ampton | Basrah |
| 22 | (various) | Martlesham Heath | 204 (FB) | South-ampton | Mount Batten |
| 23F | Gamecock | Kenley | 205 (FB) | South-ampton | Singapore |
| 24 Comm | BF, Moth and Avro 504N | Northolt | 207B | Fairey IIIF | Bircham Newton |
| | | | 208AC | BF | Helwan |
| 25F | Siskin | Hawkinge | 216B | Victoria | Heliopolis |
| 26AC | Atlas | Catterick | 501B | Avro 504N | Filton |
| 27B | DH9A | Kohat | 502B | Avro 504N | Aldergrove |
| 28AC | BF | Ambala | 503B | Hyderabad | Waddington |
| 29F | Siskin | North Weald | 504B | Horsley | Hucknall |
| 30B | Wapiti | Mosul, Iraq | 600B | Wapiti | Hendon |
| 31AC | BF | Quetta | 601B | DH9A | Hendon |
| 32F | Siskin | Kenley | 602B | Wapiti | Renfrew |
| 33B | Horsley | Eastchurch | 603B | DH9A | Turnhouse |
| 35B | DH9A | Bircham Newton | 605B | DH9A | Castle Bromwich |

RAF Cadet and Staff Colleges; Central Flying, Nos 1–5 Flying Training, Armament and Gunnery, Aircraft Co-operation, Electrical and Wireless, Photography, Technical Training (Men and Boys), Balloon Training and Accounting and Storekeeping Schools.

Notes: BF = Bristol Fighter. Nos 600 to 603 and 605 Sqns included some Avro 504Ns. Normal squadron establishment 9 + 3 reserve aircraft.

**Flagship — Iris**   The RAF, in conjunction with the Blackburn Company, introduced the Iris series for general reconnaissance in the mid-'twenties. They were larger than any previous service flying boats. The first wooden-hulled Iris I flew from 1927; this was followed by the metal-hulled Iris II which, in the autumn of 1928, took the Under-Secretary of State for Air (Sir Philip Sassoon) and the Director of Equipment (Air Cdre C. A. H. Longmore) on an inspection cruise of units in Malta, Egypt and Iraq. The production version, Iris III N238, shown above on hand-over to the RAF, entered service early in 1930 with the newly re-formed No 209 Sqn. In June 1930 two of this squadron's Irises visited Reykjavik for the Thousandth Anniversary of the Icelandic Parliament. N238, shown, broke up and sank with the loss of nine lives on 4th February 1931. All Iris's were declared obsolete September 1937.

| | |
|---|---|
| Mk I | Prototype 3 × 650hp R-R Condor III. One only (N185). |
| Mk II | N185 rebuilt with metal hull had twin instead of triple fins. |
| Mk III | Condor IIIB engines. Prototype (N238) plus two (S1263–4) production and S1593 replacement for N238. |
| Mk IV | N185 fitted with 3 × 800-hp Leopard III engines. |
| Mk V | Mk IIIs with 3 × 825-hp R-R Buzzard IIMs engines. |
| Mk VI | Re-named Perth. Four built (K3580–2 & K4011). |

**The Years of the Virginia and Bulldog**    Still of conventional World War I configuration, the Bristol Bulldog first entered service as the Bulldog II with No 3 Sqn in May 1929. Designed as a Gamecock and Siskin replacement, this single-seat fighter had a maximum speed of 174 mph and could climb to 14,000 feet in $14\frac{1}{2}$ minutes. Over three hundred were supplied to the RAF where it was the most widely used home defence fighter until 1936. The first forty-eight were withdrawn in August 1934, but the strengthened and wider wheel-based IIA and 59 Mk IIA(T) trainers were not declared obsolete until September 1937. Pictures show its function as a day and night interceptor.

The main bomber of the mid-war years was the Vickers Virginia, which replaced the Vimy. It entered service in late 1924, and successive marks had improvements to structure and power plant. Retired from squadron service in the mid-'thirties it continued as a bomber and parachute trainer until November 1941. The long fuselage is emphasized in this shot of a No 7 Sqn Virginia, and the isolated position of the tail gunner is seen in the No 10 Sqn view. Until 1934 there was no trade of air gunner, the task being carried out by an armourer who qualified for flying pay.

ROYAL AIR FORCE
DISPLAY
HENDON. SAT. 27TH JUNE

**Annual Displays**    3rd July 1920 marked the first full display of the RAF to the public. Such was its success, with forty thousand people attending, that it became an annual event at Hendon, the nearest RAF station to central London. Called the RAF Pageant 1920–24 and RAF Display from 1925, it had three objects: to familiarize the public with aviation progress, form part of the annual RAF training and support RAF charities. The annual display was discontinued after the eighteenth in 1937, Empire Air Days taking its place.

The first display of 1920 had twelve events:

1  Race for standard Avro trainers (Avro 504Ks)
2  Dog fight between Fokker DVII and Martinsyde Buzzard
3  Trick flying by SE5b (Flt Lt Noakes AFC MM)
4  Formation Flying (five Bristol Fighters and five Sopwith Snipes)
5  Exhibition Flying (Sopwith Camel)
6  Formation flying of four HP V/1500 four engined bombers and parachute descent by Miss Sylvia Boyden
7  Bristol Fighter versus two Sopwith Snipe
8  Relay race by RAF stations
9  Harry Hawker exhibiting the Sopwith Scooter
10  Kite balloon attack by Flt Lt Hazell DSO MC DFC
11  Bristol Fighters in mock trench strafe
12  Air burst bombs from Handley Page 0/400

The bright impressive posters advertising the Display were the work of RAF personnel or Air Ministry staffs, chosen in an annual competition for which prizes were awarded. In the 1936 competition the winning entry was by Group Captain R. M. Hill MC AFC, ADC who commanded Fighter Command in 1943–4, and the runner-up was E. A. Wren of No 604 (County of Middlesex) Squadron who became the famous aviation cartoonist.

**The Hendon Spectacular, 1920–37** An innovation from the 1923 Display was a New Types Park of prototype and experimental aircraft, exhibited in a static park, which usually flew to provide an event on the programme. Two new types at the 1934 Display were the Supermarine D & N fighter, a stage in the development of the Spitfire, and the Overstrand, which replaced No 101 Sqn's Sidestrands, seen respectively as New Types Nos 2 and 13.

Smoke trails always make a pleasing spectacle, and Bulldogs are seen left, with smoke canisters attached to the fuselage, practising for a display. Below, Siskins formation flying linked together at the 1930 display, with streamers attached to the connection cords.

**Bomber-transports**   Classed as bomber-transports, the Vickers Victoria and modified Valentia were the workhorse transports of the RAF in Nos 70 and 216 Sqns in the Middle East. They were used for desert searches, such as in September–October 1928 when a shooting party was lost in the Western Desert, transported bombs for punitive expeditions, carried out demonstration flights earning the nickname 'Father of aeroplanes' from the tribesmen in contrast to the single-engined types. In October 1931 they were called upon to airlift troops to Cyprus during civil disturbances and that same year supported No 14 Sqn and No 2 Armoured Car Company on tribal control operations in Palestine. Victorias of No 216 Sqn went south to Aden and Somaliland to show the flag in 1932. Some survived to the late 'thirties (as shown), and K9763 (also illustrated) was wrecked in a rough landing at Hinaidi, 11th October 1935, with only slight injuries to the crew.

**Trainers for the 'Thirties**   Designed by Hawker to break the Avro
monopoly of training aircraft, the all-metal framed Tomtit, powered by a
150-hp Armstrong Siddeley Mongoose IIIC engine, was ordered in three
batches 1929–31, totalling twenty-five aircraft, and they served mainly
as primary trainers in No 3 Flying Training School. The example shown
was attached to 'C' Flight, RAF Base Gosport. Tomtits were declared
obsolete in January 1940.

The Avro monopoly was barely affected for the Avro 504N, basically a
Lynx radial-engined version of the rotary-engined 504K, was replaced
by the Avro Tutor. An initial batch of twenty-one Mongoose-engined
Tutors, introduced in 1930 and retired in 1937, were followed by 380
Lynx IVC-engined versions. The Tutors shown are the aerobatic team of
the Central Flying School, with the lead aircraft flying inverted,
practising for the 1935 Air Display at Hendon. The Tutors were used for
liaison work during World War II and were not officially withdrawn
until October 1947.

**Fighting Colours**    Fighters were the only squadrons permitted unit markings and each chose their own. A reversion to the wartime symbols was advocated in September 1924, but that month nine fighter squadrons had decided on their markings. No 17 Sqn's was a black zig-zag, as seen above on their Bulldogs in 1930, and below the black lines adopted by No 25 Sqn are seen on their Fury IIs, 29th May 1937. During this period rudder striping had changed from blue, white and red from the rudder post, to the reverse order in 1930, and in 1934 rudder striping was discontinued altogether to avoid painting on control surfaces. Wheel discs were painted in red, yellow and blue for 'A', 'B' and 'C' flights respectively from December 1924. The appropriate colours were also used by flight commanders on the fins of their aircraft as seen on the Fury K7270. Squadron badges were regulated by the Office of Chester Herald who was appointed Inspector of RAF Badges 1st March 1935. These badges could be displayed on fins within a frame differing according to the unit role. Fighter squadrons had a spearhead frame as illustrated, bomber squadrons a grenade form and others a six-point star. These unit markings were not normally used on camouflaged finishes, introduced on the Hurricane from 1937, and were overpainted in the Munich crisis of 1938 on all fighters. Unit markings were then replaced by unit code letters.

The RAF worked closely with the Royal Aircraft Establishment, Farnborough, on many devices and improvements, including early flight refuelling experiments with a Virginia the tanker and a Wapiti the receiver. The experiments reached fruition postwar with Flight Refuelling Ltd co-operating with the RAF.

The Cierva C30A autogyro, built under licence by Avro, entered RAF service at the School of Army Co-operation in December 1934 as the world's first service STOL (short take-off and landing) aircraft. Known as the Rota in RAF service it was used in army co-operation experiments. Surviving Rotas were impressed during World War II for radar calibration duties.

**RAF College, Cranwell**   The first line Hawker biplanes of the early
and mid-'thirties, Harts, Audax and Hinds, continued in production, and
ex-squadron aircraft were converted to trainers in the late 'thirties for
the large Volunteer Reserve aircraft entry. Above are a flight of Audax
trainers of the RAF College seen on 22nd May 1938. The College had
opened at Cranwell on 5th February 1920, using wartime hutted
accommodation until 1934 when the present building was opened by the
Prince of Wales. Accommodation was for 150 cadets in three wings,
behind the building shown below, with space for an additional wing. By
World War II there had been forty-four successive entries to produce the
RAF's élite, 1,095 officers trained as pilots.

**The Royal Review, 1935**    In the Jubilee Year of his reign, King George V accompanied by TRH the Prince of Wales and Duke of York, arrived at the newly-opened RAF station Mildenhall at 11.00 hrs to review units as charted overleaf, a total of 356 aircraft in serried rows, crews in front of aircraft, squadron and flight commanders in advance. Accompanied by Air Chief Marshal Sir H. Brooke Popham, the royal party reviewed from an open car, while the band of the RAF College Cranwell played on the tarmac.

At 1215 hrs the royal party left for Duxford, where they mounted a dais at 1425 hrs for the largest flypast the world had ever known.

**Order of Flypast in line abreast**          *Overhead Duxford 1430 hrs*
**Phase 1**

| Flypast Groups | Squadron Nos in order of flypast | Speed (mph) | No of Aircraft |
|---|---|---|---|
| No 1 Heavy Bomber | 99, 10 | 98 | 20 |
| No 2 Light Bomber | 57, 15, 18, 142 | 115 | 36 |
| No 3 Army Co-op | 12, 2, 26, 23 | 115 | 36 |
| No 4 Fighter | 3, 17, 111, 32, 54, 56 | 120 | 34 |
| No 5 Fighter | 1, 25, 43, 19 | 150 | 36 |

2 spans between aircraft. 500 yds between squadrons. 2 miles between groups.

**Phase 2**    No 19 Sqn Gauntlets in flying drill display.
**Phase 3**    Seventeen squadrons having made wide circle, fly past again in wing formation. 155 aircraft at 1,200 feet. Finish 1500 hrs.

Most modern of the bombers in the flypast was the RAF's last biplane bomber, the Handley Page Heyford that entered service with No 99 Sqn at Upper Heyford in November 1933. In all, 124 of three versions were delivered to the RAF, and the type was replaced in squadron service by 1939 and declared obsolete in 1941. Mk I of No 99 Sqn shown.

Photo taken during the form-up at Mildenhall.

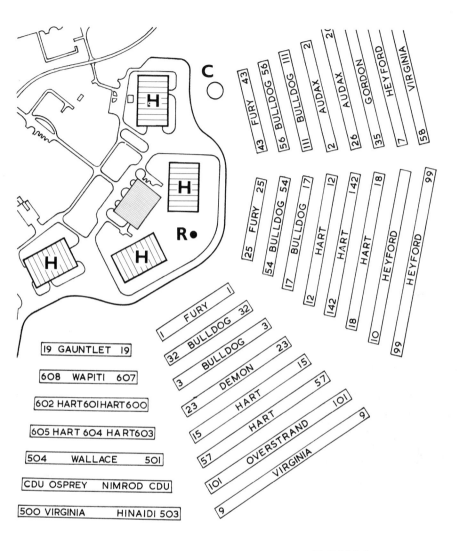

FURY 43 43
BULLDOG 56 56
BULLDOG III III
AUDAX 2 2
AUDAX 26
GORDON 35
HEYFORD 7
VIRGINIA 58

FURY 25 25
BULLDOG 54 54
BULLDOG 17 17
HART 12 12
HART 142 142
HART 18 18
HEYFORD 10
HEYFORD 99 99

C

H

H

R●

H H

I FURY I
32 BULLDOG 32
3 BULLDOG 3
23 DEMON 23
I5 HART I5
57 HART 57
IOI OVERSTRAND IOI
9 VIRGINIA 9

19 GAUNTLET 19

608 WAPITI 607

602 HART 60I HART 600

605 HART 604 HART 603

504 WALLACE 50I

CDU OSPREY NIMROD CDU

500 VIRGINIA HINAIDI 503

# ROYAL
# REVIEW PLAN
*Squadrons and
Aircraft Types
RAF Mildenhall*

C    COMPASS SWINGING POINT

R    ROYAL STANDARD

H    HANGARS

CDU    COAST DEFENCE UNIT

NUMERALS RELATE TO SQUADRON NUMBERS

**The Quetta Disaster** "My wife was awakened by a roar like that of a very large underground train coming into a station and by our bedroom behaving like a small boat in a rough sea," wrote Marshal of the RAF Sir John Slessor (then Station Commander Quetta) of the moments at 03.00 hrs on Friday, 31st May 1935, when an earthquake at Quetta inflicted the heaviest casualties the RAF suffered in the inter-war years. A thick pall of dust hung over the camp, obscuring the extent of the damage. In the wrecked buildings shown opposite before and after the disaster, fifty-four RAF personnel, sixty-six Indian other ranks, and two children were crushed to death and some two hundred were injured.

The hangars had not collapsed, but not one of No 5 Sqn's Wapitis was serviceable, and the squadron reformed at Chaklala. No 31 Sqn's hangar doors had jammed and were ripped open by tanks to reveal only three serviceable Wapitis, but this permitted reconnaissance and sending for assistance; the squadron reformed at Drigh Road. After the rescue operations, aided by a flight of Victorias for casualty evacuation, the station was wired off and abandoned.

**India 1935** India Command that year had been involved in Momand operations. Up to thirty-eight aircraft had been put into the air at one time to impress the populace, and an economic blockade of the Momands moving towards the plains had involved night flying. For the first time since Handley Pages had been experimentally flown to India, Valentias that year were delivered by air; previously aircraft had been crated and shipped.

Quetta (now in Pakistan) had been an important station on the North-West Frontier of India, where Westland Wapitis had become the standard general purpose aircraft of the 'thirties. Wapiti J9743 of No 27 Sqn is seen below bombed up at Miranshah in 1930 when some seventy-five tons of bombs were dropped in action against Afridis. The 550-hp Bristol Jupiter engine is being run up, prior to the chocks being removed for take-off. This aircraft subsequently served in No 20 Sqn and completed fifteen hundred hours of flying in India.

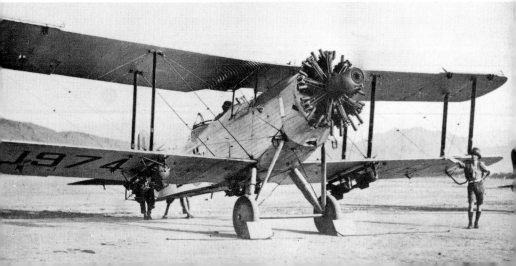

**Hey-day of the Biplane**   The Gladiator, successor to the Gauntlet and the RAF's last biplane fighter, introduced an enclosed cockpit and four ·303 Browning guns in place of the Gauntlet's two ·303 Vickers – the armament of fighters when the RAF formed in 1918. The Gladiator equipped fourteen regular and five auxiliary squadrons at home and a few overseas. Introduced in January 1937 and withdrawn from squadrons after 1940, it was not declared obsolete until May 1945, having been used during the war first as a fighter and then on meteorological duties.

Hawker Hart day bombers, powered by a Rolls-Royce Kestrel engine, predominated in RAF service in the mid-'thirties. Variants included the army co-operation Audax with message pick-up hook, Hardy general purpose aircraft for overseas, Hind light bomber and the Demon two-seat fighter (as shown below of No 23 Sqn) with a Frazer Nash turret.

The Air Ministry took control of the Meteorological Office on 1st July 1919, and in the 'twenties some ten civil meteorological stations were maintained at RAF stations. During the 'thirties Met Flights were formed for daily atmosphere sampling; a Gauntlet of the Duxford Met Flight is seen *circa* 1938. The Gauntlet, which equipped fifteen regular and five auxiliary squadrons at home 1935–8 – and a few overseas, continued after squadron service in various roles until February 1944.

King George V and Queen Mary on a station inspection at Bircham Newton 24th May 1935 with (centre) the station commander who became AV-M R. Collishaw CB DSO OBE DSC DFC, famous for shooting down sixty enemy aircraft in World War I. Left to right are lines of Gordons, a Fury and a Tutor (extreme right).

**The Abyssinian Crisis**   The Fairey Gordon was a basic Fairey IIIF (shown earlier) but with a radial engine (525-hp Armstrong Siddeley Panther IIA) that served in three squadrons at home and four overseas in the 'thirties and then as a communications aircraft from 1931 until June 1944. These Gordons of No 47 Sqn in the Sudan had an Eritrean and Abyssinian border patrolling role.

The Italian invasion of Abyssinia in late 1935 brought Britain to the brink of war, and the RAF in the Near and Middle East was strengthened by squadrons from Britain, plus a detachment of No 22 Sqn's Vickers Vildebeest III torpedo bombers (shown) which moved to Malta.

**Palestinian Disturbances**   Britain's unhappy burden of the Palestinian Mandate was carried out on behalf of the League of Nations. Conflict between Arab and Jew brought murder, arson, sabotage and crop destruction. The Harts of Nos 6 (one seen above Jerusalem, March 1937) and 33 Sqns and a flight of Gordons of No 14 Sqn were continually on call for dispersing concentrations of irregular forces. On 3rd September 1936 a Hart of No 6 Sqn crashed killing both crew members. A few days later Hart K4471 force landed after being damaged in flight; it is seen being salvaged by a six-wheeled Morris tender crew under the protection of an RAF armoured car.

**The Middle East Base, mid-'thirties**   Heliopolis, an RAF station in Egypt, on parade in 1937. This station was the base of No 216 (Bomber Transport) Sqn whose nine Vickers Valentias are seen at the top of the circle. Following round clock-wise are five Fairey Gordons of a detached flight of No 14 (Bomber) Sqn and the Audax of No 208 (Army Co-op) Sqn complete the circle. The Middle East was the RAF's central reserve, with its own flying training school (No 4), and practice reinforcing

flights were made to Malta, Aden and Iraq from time to time. The Command in 1937 were mainly concerned with civic duties, delivering smallpox serum to various African colonies and conducting air searches on several occasions for civil aircraft and parties lost in the desert. While the entire force was composed of biplanes in 1937, re-equipment of the bomber squadrons started in 1938 with Wellesleys.

**Iraq . . .** Disturbances in Iraq continued. Riots in 1931 led to a police airlift and demonstrations by No 55 Sqn. The following year Assyrian Levies rebelled, leading to Victorias being concentrated at Ismailia to airlift 562 troops into Iraq. This was followed by the Barzan operations to force the submission of Sheikh Ahmed and rebel leaders, involving thirty Wapitis of Nos 30 and 55 Sqns and ten Victorias of No 70 Sqn dropping $32 \times 520$-lb, $555 \times 112$-lb and $6,822 \times 20$-lb bombs and firing 98,448 rounds. Two airmen were killed, another died of wounds and two others, plus an officer, were wounded in the campaign. In the first half of 1933 an Assyrian revolt caused an airlift of six hundred Levy dependants. Hardys replaced the Wapitis in No 30 Sqn in 1935, and one is shown above the a guard of No 8 Company, Iraq Levies, operating under RAF command. With tribal trouble in India and Aden, and conflict between Arab and Jew in Palestine, it was as well that Iraq was relatively quiet in the late 'thirties. Below, Vincents of No 55 Sqn are seen on a message pick-up exercise in Iraq.

**... Aden and Transjordan** Indicative of action in Aden in the
'thirties – a bombed-up Vincent of No 8 Sqn. As early as 1919 Snipes had
demonstrated in the Yemen to secure the release of a Mission, and a
permanent flight at Aden, under Army command, acted against raiding
Yemeni tribes from the early 'twenties. In 1927 No 8 Sqn (DH9As)
moved to Khormaksar, Aden, and in February 1928 the Protectorate
was made an RAF responsibility. Co-operating with RAF armoured cars,
No 8 Sqn flew against Zeidi Imam involving a thousand flying hours in
seven months dropping nearly fifty tons of bombs. Zeidi incursions
caused further trouble in 1933 when the squadron re-equipped with
Fairey IIIFs, used also in 1934 against the Quteribi tribe.

There was an investigation in 1935 after tribes claimed that firing at
aircraft was a form of greeting! That year four Fairey IIIFs of No 8 Sqn
made a flight to West Africa. During the Abyssinian crisis, No 12 Sqn
(Harts) and No 41 Sqn (Demons) were sent to Aden, but they returned
to England in 1936.

No 14 Sqn was based in Transjordan at Amman 1926–39, their Gordons
being seen over the territory in 1937. They were often called into action
in Palestine where in 1938 fifty-eight aircraft were hit by ground fire,
and nine were destroyed.

**Record Flying: Distance, Height and Speed**   Two Fairey long-range monoplanes were built for RAF distance record breaking. J9479 in April 1929 made the first non-stop England (Cranwell) to India (Karachi) flight in under 51 hours. Unfortunately it crashed in Tunisia on a long-distance record attempt to South Africa. The second, K1991 refined with an automatic pilot, set up a World Distance Record of 5,309 miles in 52 hours 25 minutes, 6th–8th February 1933, flying non-stop from Cranwell to Walvis Bay, South Africa. The crew were Sqn Ldr O. R. Gayford and Flt Lt G. E. Nicholetts.

A world altitude record for the RAF flying the Bristol 138A was made on 28th September 1936. Sqn Ldr F. R. D. Swain took K4879 up to 49,967 feet from Farnborough and landed at Netheravon, having broken the world altitude record held by France. When Italy broke the record in May 1937, Flt Lt M. J. Adam took the 138A up to 53,937 feet on 30th June 1937 to regain the record for Britain.

The Schneider maritime trophy contest captured the public imagination. The Air Ministry issued a specification for a high-speed aircraft in 1926 and the RAF first entered a team in the 1927 Tenth Contest at Venice, winning with Flt Lt S. N. Webster averaging 281·49 mph in a Napier-engined Supermarine S5 floatplane. The 1929 contest was again won by the RAF representing Britain against Italy, the only other competitor, with Flg Off H. R. D. Waghorn averaging 328·63 mph in a Rolls-Royce-engined Supermarine S6. After which, on 12th September, Sqn Ldr A. H. Orlebar raised the World's Speed Record to 336·3 mph and later to 357·7 mph. The 12th Contest, which Lady Houston prodded the Air Ministry into entering by her financial support, was uncontested. Flt Lt J. W. Boothman, in Supermarine S6B S1595 illustrated, flew the required seven laps on 13th September 1931 to fulfil the conditions of three successive British wins for our permanent retention of the Trophy. On the 29th Flt Lt G. H. Stainforth set up a World Speed Record on S1595 of 407·5 mph.

Evaluation of a wide range of aircraft was carried out at Martlesham Heath, the Aeroplane Experimental Station, re-named Aeroplane and Armament Experimental Station from 1924, where, ten years later, are left to right: AW19, DH Gipsy Moth, Vought Corsair and Northrop 2E.

**Force Expansion, 1934–7**   The Prime Minister, Stanley Baldwin, gave assurances to the country in March 1934 that if the Disarmament Conferences failed, steps would be taken to bring the RAF up to the strength of the strongest air force within striking distance of the UK. This expansion was announced the following June. Squadrons at home would be increased from fifty-two to seventy-five bringing total RAF strength to 128 squadrons.

With Nazi Germany a growing threat to European peace, and Italian aspirations in Africa, a further expansion was approved in July 1936, due for completion by March 1939. There were five main objectives:

1.  Increase Metropolitan Force to 124 Squadrons with front-line strength of 1,736 aircraft and particularly the striking power of the bomber squadrons.

2.  To add ten squadrons to overseas garrisons, additional to those approved under previous scheme.

3.  To form two new regular and four auxiliary army co-operation squadrons.

4.  To increase the number of aircraft in the Fleet Air Arm.

5.  Provide passive air defence of sensitive areas by a Balloon Barrage.

On 14th July a new command structure of the RAF came into force with the introduction of Bomber, Fighter, Coastal and Training Commands.

Under the 1934 Scheme some 2,500 pilots and 27,000 airmen were required to be trained in under two years. The 1936 Scheme approved a total entry of 3,779 pilots (officers and airmen), 36,384 airmen, apprentices and boys. At the end of July 1936 the RAF Volunteer Reserve was formed to train eight hundred pilots a year.

Advertisements appeared in daily papers and magazines and recruiting depots were raised to ten, located in London, Belfast, Birmingham, Cardiff, Glasgow, Leeds, Liverpool, Manchester, Newcastle and Plymouth.

Enlistments of men and boys April 1935 to the end of 1936 were:

| | | | |
|---|---|---|---|
| Skilled fitters | 1,003 | Apprentices for fitter, armourers, wireless | |
| For training as flight mechanics and riggers | 5,421 | mechanics, instrument makers and clerks | 3,093 |
| For training as wireless/operator, armourer and photographer | 2,352 | Boy entrants for wireless operator, armourer and photographer | 952 |
| Various ground and domestic trades | 8,131 | | |
| Total men recruits | 16,907 | Total boy entrants | 4,045 |

The first units to be formed were, of necessity, training units, and five new (Nos 7–11) Flying Training Schools were opened in 1935. For *ab initio* flying training thirteen civil flying training schools were co-opted. Nine new Armament Training Camps (re-named Armament Training Stations in April 1938) were needed and a comprehensive search of the coastlines of Britain was made with protests from a dozen societies, delaying the acquisition of sites.

The striking power of the Bomber Squadrons was to be achieved by:

1. The formation of twenty-seven new regular and three new auxiliary bomber squadrons by April 1937.

2. Increasing the number of aircraft of light bomber squadrons from 12 + 3 reserve to 16 + 5 reserve.

3. Re-arming a number of squadrons with aircraft of increased speed, range and carrying capacity, viz Battle, Blenheim, Hampden, Harrow, Whitley, Wellesley and Wellington.

During 1937 over thirty new aerodromes, with hangars and technical accommodation being given priority over domestic sites; this was, at most locations, of a temporary nature, mainly Air Ministry Huts Type 'A' & 'B'. This decision was wholly justified by events as the accommodation that followed comprised well-built structures – barrack blocks, messes and institutes, still in excellent condition today.

The RAF's first turretted bomber and the only twin-engined day bomber in the mid-'thirties was the Boulton and Paul Overstrand, which replaced the Sidestrand in No 101 Sqn from 1935, seen here in 'V' formation, 1936. Used later for gunnery training, Overstrands were finally declared obsolete in November 1941.

**Empire Air Days, 1934–7**   Empire Air Days were held on a Saturday in May each year from 1934 to 1939, when numbers of RAF stations were open to the public. This is scene at Castle Bromwich, one of forty-four stations open on 23rd May 1936. RAF aircraft on the field are Furys, Harts, Wapitis, Bulldogs, a Heyford and Overstrand, while bottom right civil aircraft run flips at 5/- (25p) a flight. In those days, when visitors went by rail rather than road, Hornchurch held the attendance record with 14,570, to Biggin Hill's mere 6,940. Popularity of the open days increased, and total attendances rose from 77,000 in 1934 to 350,000 in 1937.

Just one hundred Handley Page Harrows were built, equipping five bomber squadrons from January 1937. Impressive-looking craft, although only interim equipment, examples were distributed to stations open on Empire Air Days 1937–9. The Harrow, withdrawn as a bomber in 1939, was used for transport and special duties until July 1945.

Below: a crowd at Kenley watch a Demon, in the red and blue checks of No 23 Sqn, test its guns at the butts, during an Empire Air Day Display. The last Empire Air Day in 1939 attracted nearly a million people to the sixty-two RAF stations and fifteen civil airfields open. RAF charities, selected by the Air Ministry, benefited by some £30,000. The largest share went to the RAF Benevolent Fund, known prior to 1934 as the RAF Memorial Fund.

**Eight-gun Fighters Arrive**   The Hawker Hurricane entered service with No 111 Sqn at Northolt in December 1937 and the Supermarine Spitfire with No 19 Sqn at Duxford from August 1938. These first service monoplane fighters were also the first with retractable undercarriages, and they doubled the armament of former fighters. They had a common factor of a Rolls-Royce Merlin and both featured eight guns. The Hurricane is seen above with a demonstration of the ammunition belts for Browning guns, being fired by a Spitfire below at the butts. An important difference, emphasized in these views, was that the Hurricane's undercarriage retracted inward and the Spitfire's outward, necessitating a smaller wheel-track on the Spitfire.

**Long-range Bombers Introduced**    The longest non-stop flight by a complete RAF unit was accomplished on 8th July 1938 after four Vickers Wellesleys of the Long Range Development Unit had left Cranwell on the 7th and landed at Ismailia after thirty-two hours continuous flying, 4,300 miles distant. The unit, commanded by Sqn Ldr R. G. Kellett, went back to Ismailia and, three aircraft set out for Darwin on 5th November. Two of the Wellesleys set up a world's distance record by 7,162 miles in their flight to Australia, but the third forced landed at Koepang *en route*. While there were special long-range aircraft, such as L2637 shown above, standard Wellesleys equipped six squadrons at home from April 1937 – one is shown below with a supply pannier fitted. In 1938 it became policy to withdraw the Wellesleys from Bomber Command due to their inadequate defence of two ·303 machine-guns, and they were sent for store in the Middle East where later four squadrons (Nos 14, 45, 47 and 233) were maintained, and they operated in East Africa against the Italians. Wellesleys were also used for special reconnaissance work in the Middle East, operating from Malta, and were finally declared obsolete for all service purposes in August 1943.

# ROYAL AIR FORCE DISPOSITIONS

### DAWN 1st SEPTEMBER 1939

Map by arrangement with Aeromilitaria of Air Britain.

**Battle strength, 1939**    The map opposite shows RAF stations functioning at the outbreak of war, 3rd September 1939. Aircraft strength in squadrons was as follows:

Bombers: 160 Wellingtons, 140 Whitleys, 169 Hampdens, 338 Blenheims and 529 Battles. In addition three Harrows and small number of Heyfords awaited transfer to Maintenance Units.

Fighters: 347 Hurricanes, 187 Spitfires, 111 Blenheims, 76 Gladiators and 26 Gauntlets.

Coastal landplanes: 301 Ansons, 53 Hudsons, 30 Vildebeests.

Flying boats: 27 Sunderlands, 17 Londons, 9 Stranraers.

Army Co-op: 95 Lysanders, 9 Hectors, 46 Hinds.

Training schools were equipped with some five hundred Oxfords, Harvards, Harts and Tiger Moths. In addition there were Tiger Moths, Blackburn B2 and miscellaneous training types at Elementary and Reserve Flying Training Schools at non-operational airfields.

Miscellaneous aircraft included Mentors, Vega Gulls and Magisters for communications and Henleys and Wallaces for anti-aircraft co-operation and target-towing.

Immediately following the declaration of war, there was a reshuffle of units at stations as squadrons left for France.

Stalwart of Coastal Command, the Avro Anson was the first operational monoplane when it entered service in March 1936 with No 48 Sqn at Manston whose Anson Is are seen on war service. Ansons were the first aircraft to become operational in World War II and an Anson of No 500 Sqn made the first RAF attack on a U-boat on 5th September 1939.

**Hudson and Hampden**  Ordered pre-war in June 1938 in quantity (two hundred) together with an equal number of Harvard trainers, the Lockheed Hudson was the first America-built aircraft to see operations in World War II being used by RAF Coastal Command from the summer of 1939. It was used at home and overseas on maritime reconnaissance, convoy protection, special support duties, as transports and meteorological tasks, until withdrawn in September 1945. Pictures show the aircraft's main defence, twin ·303 machine-guns in a dorsal turret, and bombing up for anti-shipping duties.

The Pegasus-engined Handley Page Hampden, coming into service at the time of the Munich crisis, equipped eight Bomber Command squadrons when war came. It failed in early daylight raids but operated at night until September 1942. A Napier Dagger in-line engined version, the Hereford, failed to become operational and was declared obsolete in May 1942. The following month a torpedo-carrying version of the Hampden was introduced for shipping strikes, giving it a new lease of life in Coastal Command. Some were flown to Canada (where, incidentally, 180 were built) for operational training duties. The type was finally declared obsolete in August 1944, and not one has survived.

**Heavy and Medium Bombers.**   The Whitley (above), classed as a long-range night bomber, came into service in March 1937 and was operational in Bomber Command until 30th August 1942. The Blenheim (below) entered service in March 1937 with No 113 Sqn in its Mk 1 (Short-nosed) version and was superseded by the Mk IV (Long-nosed) version. Until 1938 bombers carried their unit number on the fuselage side with an individual letter for identification, hence K 10 on the Whitley. From 1938 code letters were issued instead of the unit numbers and were changed when war was declared for security reasons, but from then on there was little change; No 110 Sqn, whose Blenheims led the first attack of World War II, were allotted VE (as seen below). The Blenheim I served operationally in the Middle and Far East and was withdrawn mid-1944, and the Mk IV and V (the latter widely used in the Western Desert) a year later.

**Army Co-operation and Light Bombers**    Probably the best-known
and certainly the easiest to recognize of all RAF aircraft was the
Lysander. Their army co-operation task entailed up to ten Army officers
attached to each squadron as well as two Miles Mentors on the
establishment – one for army liaison and one for training. These units
were fully mobile, with tented accommodation when on exercises, and
they were responsible for their own local defence at a time before an RAF
Regiment existed. Picture shows a turn-round of a Lysander at the
School of Army Co-operation.

Introduced in May 1937 with No 63 Sqn at Andover, the Fairey Battle
became the standard light bomber equipping some twenty squadrons
(example of No 15 Sqn shown). During 1939 the Hawker Hart variants
in operational units and station flights were replaced by Battles,
releasing the Hawker aircraft for Volunteer Reserve training. By March
1939 each regular Hurricane and Spitfire squadron had a Battle on
strength fitted with dual control. Altogether 1,160 were built, and after
its failure on operations in 1940 it was delegated to training, including
target-towing. All versions were declared obsolete in July 1944.

**Balloon Command, 1938–40**   Barrage balloon squadrons, formed under the Expansion Scheme, went to war stations in the Munich crisis and were deployed from 27th September to 8th October 1938. No 30 Balloon Group of Fighter Command became Balloon Command from 1st November 1938 and expanded with Auxiliary Air Force squadrons as listed with the number of balloons operated.

| | | |
|---|---|---:|
| No 30 Group | 901 to 903 (County of London) | 135 |
| Squadrons | 904 and 905 (County of Surrey) | 90 |
| | 906 and 907 (County of Middlesex) | 90 |
| | 908 to 910 (County of Essex) | 135 |
| No 31 Group | 911 to 917 (County of Warwick) | 200 |
| Squadrons | 918 (County of Derby) | 24 |
| | 919 to 921 (West Lancashire) | 88 |
| | 922 and 923 (West Lancashire) | 64 |
| | 924 to 926 (East Lancashire) | 80 |
| No 32 Group | 927 to 929 (County of Gloucester) | 72 |
| Squadrons | 930 to 933 (Hampshire) | 96 |
| | 934 (County of Devon) | 40 |
| | 935 (County of Glamorgan) | 16 |
| No 33 Group | 936 to 938 (County of Northumberland) | 88 |
| Squadrons | 939 to 941 (West Riding) | 72 |
| | 942 to 944 (East Riding) | 72 |
| | 945 to 947 (City of Glasgow) | 88 |

Balloons were operated from lighters as shown below, but mainly from vehicles seen right in the balloon shed at Cardington.

**"Phoney War", 1939–40** Crews of Fairey Battles talk with French airmen with whom they share an airfield in France (left), and (below) a Blenheim IV of No 139 Sqn at dispersal at Betheniville, France, in the winter of 1939–40 during the so-called "Phoney War" period. This picture was taken from behind the camouflage net at a dispersal point. Both views are reproduced from a range of approved postcards which airmen were permitted to send home from France.

Gas was still considered a grave possibility, and special anti-gas clothing was issued to RAF sentries and look-outs in France. During the hard winter of the "Phoney War" 1939–40, an RAF snow-clearing party is seen at work early in 1940 clearing a runway for a Blenheim I at Croydon outside hangars that bordered Purley Way.

## British Air Forces France, 1939–40

The day before war was declared the first echelon (10 Sqns) of the Advanced Air Striking Force (AASF) under Air Vice-Marshal P. H. L. Playfair flew to France followed by the main body on surface transport. The Air Component of the British Expeditionary Force (BEF) under Air Vice-Marshal C. H. B. Blount followed and functioned from 15th September.

Administrative difficulties in liaison with the French, the allocation of airfields and equipment supply (eg No 21 Aircraft Depot administered by the AASF was responsible for equipment supplies to both AASF and the Air Component) led to an overall RAF Command, British Air Forces France (BAFF) from 15th January 1940 under Air Marshal A. S. Barratt. A large airfield building plan was put in hand with concrete runways being made, but few sites were operational by the evacuation of France in May and June.

The Air Component squadrons were fully mobile but the ancillary units and the AASF in general were only partially mobile, which hampered movements after the night of 9th/10th May when Germany invaded Belgium, Holland and Luxembourg. The twelve AASF squadrons, based in the Rheims area, were supplemented almost immediately by a further Hurricane squadron and became embroiled in intensive operations against the German advance. Reacting in conjunction with the BEF, the Air Component was quickly reinforced by three Hurricane squadrons and thirty-two crews. But crippling losses were suffered; on 14th May alone, when sixty-seven Blenheims and Battles were sent out against road and bridge targets in the Sedan area, thirty-five failed to return.

A rear HQ for the Air Component was hastily formed at Hawkinge from which reconnaissance and fighter support was directed, and an HQ was flown to Rouen on 21st May to co-ordinate units in the area.

Hundreds of vehicles were supplied by the French for the rapid redeployments required in the face of the German advance, but it was impossible to move all stores and equipment. Some six million gallons of British aviation fuel, plus emergency holdings of French fuel, were dispersed over wide areas; this was but one commodity requiring movement or destruction to prevent its falling in enemy hands.

BRITISH AIR FORCES FRANCE    HQ Nantes                    May 10th 1940
No 2 Base Area HQ and No 21 Aircraft Depot, Nantes
No 98 Sqn of Battles in reserve at Nantes
Nos 1–10 Port Detachments of which seven were operating.

ADVANCED AIR STRIKING FORCE (AASF)     HQ Rheims       May 10th 1940

| Wing | Sqn Nos | Aircraft | Location |
|------|---------|----------|----------|
| 67 | 1, 73 | 32 Hurricanes | Vassincourt and Rouvres |
| 71 | 114, 139 | 36 Blenheim | Vraux and Plivot |
| 71 | 105, 150 | 36 Battles | Villeneuve and Ecury |
| 75 | 88, 103, 218 | 52 Battles | Mourmelon, Betheniville and Auberive |
| 76 | 12, 142, 226 | 52 Battles | Amifontaine, Berry au Bac and Rheims |

No 212 Sqn at Tigeaux came directly under HQ for reconnaissance
No 1 Regional Control Station Villeneuve
No 2 Salvage Unit, Mourmelon
No 62 Wing Servicing Unit, St Hilaire le Grand
Nos 4–6 Air Stores Parks, Ludes, Verzenay and Avise
Forward Air Ammunition Park, Ormes
'M' Balloon Unit, Mareuil sur Ay
Nos 1 and 2 Heavy Mobile W/T Sections, Grauves and Cuts
Nos 1 and 2 Medical Receiving Stations, Prosnes and Mareuil
Nos 1–6 Servicing Flight Sections at various locations.
Various attached Army Units.

AIR COMPONENT    *HQ Maroeuil*            May 10th 1940

| Wing | Sqn Nos | Aircraft | Location | Function |
|------|---------|----------|----------|----------|
| 50 | 4 and 13 | 36 Lysanders | Mons-en-Chaussee | Army co-operation |
| 50 | 16 | 16 Lysanders | Bertangles | Army co-operation |
| '51 | 2 and 26 | 36 Lysanders | Abbeville and St Aubin | Army co-operation |
| 52 | 53 and 59 | 36 Blenheims | near Poix | Strategic recce |
| 60 | 85 and 87 | 32 Hurricanes | Seclin | Fighter |
| 61 | 607, 615 | 32 Hurricanes | Vitry | Fighter |
| 70 | 18, 57 | 36 Blenheims | Meharicourt | Night recce |

No 81 (Communications) Sqn at Amiens came directly under HQ
Nos 1, 2 and 3 Repair Salvage Units, Amiens, Abbeville and Rosières
No 63 Wing Servicing Unit, Merville and Seclin.
Northern Wireless Intelligence Screen with twelve posts
1st Air Formation Signals, Royal Corps of Signals at various locations
HQ No 1 (Balloon) Wing: No 912 and 924 Sqns Boulogne and Le Havre.
No 5 Signals Wing* with No 1 Filter Centre, Arras, Nos 1–6 Radio
Direction Finding and Nos 1–3 Air Raid Reporting Liaison Sections.
No 1 RAF Station, Amiens Glisy, No 2 Regional Control Station*, Vitry.
No 3 British Air Mission*, Valenciennes
* Administrative control only.

**The Battle of Britain, 1940**

Before the Battle – Fighter Command, 10th July 1940

| Station | Squadrons | Aircraft | Station | Squadrons | Aircraft |
|---|---|---|---|---|---|
| *No 10 Group,* HQ Box Wilts | | | *No 12 Group,* HQ Watnell, Notts | | |
| Exeter | 87,213 | Hurricane | Coltishall | 66 | Spitfire |
| Pembrey | 92 | Spitfire | Debden | 17,85 | Hurricane |
| St Eval | 234 | Spitfire | Digby | 29,46, 64 | Blen/Hur/Spit |
| *No 11 Group,* HQ Uxbridge, Middx | | | Duxford | 19,264 | Spit/Defiant |
| Biggin Hill | 32,79 | Hurricane | Kirton-in- | 222,253 | Spit/Hurr |
| Croydon | 111,501 | Hurricane | Lindsey | | |
| Gravesend | 610 | Spitfire | Wittering | 23,229,266 | Blen/Hurr/Spit |
| Hawkinge | 245 | Hurricane | *No 13 Group,* HQ Newcastle-on-Tyne | | |
| Hornchurch | 65,74 | Spitfire | Acklington | 72,152 | Spitfire |
| Kenley | 64,615 | Spit/Hurr | Catterick | 41,219 | Spit/Blen |
| Manston | 600 | Blenheim | Drem | 602 | Spitfire |
| Martlesham | 25 | Blenheim | Leconfield | 249,616 | Hurr/Spit |
| Middle Wallop | 236 | Blenheim | Montrose | 603('B' Flt only) | Spitfire |
| Northolt | 1,604,609 | Hurr/Blen/ Spit | Turnhouse | 141,603 (A Flt) | Defiant/Spit |
| North Weald | 56,151 | Hurricane | Wick | 3,504 | Hurricane |
| Tangmere* | 43,145,601 | Hurricane | | | |

* Also Fighter Interceptor Unit with Blenheims

**Control and Reporting**   A winning factor was the organization of the reporting and control system to Sector Centres by co-ordinating RDF (later known as radar), Observer Corps (given Royal prefix on 8th May 1941) posts, anti-aircraft guns and the balloon barrage, enabling the plotting of enemy and own formations in a form that could be presented for the battle to be controlled. The No 11 Group underground Operations Room at Uxbridge was restored to its 1940 state in 1976 and is seen opposite with Wg Cdr R. R. Stanford Tuck DSO DFC, a flight commander during the Battle, facing the controller's dais watching tellers. The first phase of the Battle (8th–18th August) was mainly confined to shipping and coastal targets, then came a switch to airfields (9th August–6th September) and from then London was the main target, with day attacks gradually giving way to night attacks in October, following the first RAF attack on Berlin by eighty-one aircraft on the night of 25th/26th August. The peak day was 15th August with widespread attacks from Newcastle to Weymouth when the Luftwaffe lost ninety aircraft and the RAF lost forty-four fighters from air actions and fourteen bombers on the ground. The climax and turning point came on 15th September, now regarded annually as "Battle of Britain Day".

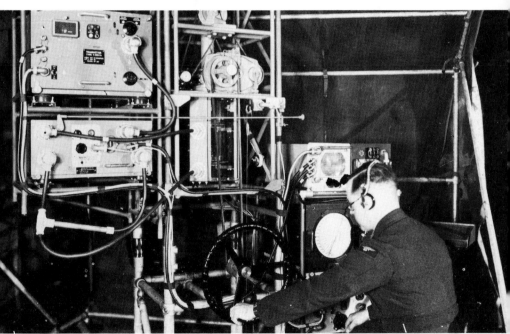

The British radar chain grew from CH (Chain Home) stations, also known as Air Ministry Experimental Stations Type 1 (AMES1), at Bawdsey, Dover and Canewdon, operational in 1937, to a chain stretching around Britain in 1940. The high towers were conspicuous but proved difficult to put out of action. New radars were introduced under the impetus of war, and a controller is shown operating the aerial winch on an early night-warning mobile radar (Type 6 T3154A) housed in a tent.

**Volunteers, Conscripts . . .**
Extracts from *A Guide for Airmen on joining the RAF*
(Air Ministry Pamphlet 130 – October 1941)

Daily Routine Orders as printed from day to day are for your information – READ THEM.

Don't play cards for money. Gambling is forbidden.

Don't bring food or intoxicating liquor into the barrack hut.

Don't light the stove before 1600 hrs unless permission IS FIRST GIVEN by the Medical Authorities.

Don't make down your bed before 1200 hrs unless you are ordered to do so.

You must have a bath *at least once each week* and must sign the bath-book if one is kept by NCO i/c Hut.

Airmen leaving camp must always be properly dressed and must carry both respirator and steel helmet.

The practice of airmen assembling at main road junctions and signalling motorists, is forbidden.

Normally you will not be granted any leave while you are under training, but exceptionally compassionate cases will receive sympathetic consideration. When you have completed your training you may be granted seven days' leave every three months if you can be spared from your duties. You may, in addition to your ordinary leave, be allowed a pass up to forty-eight hours from time to time at the discretion of your unit or station commander.

NAAFI Institutes are provided at nearly all stations and contain a restaurant, a games room, a reading room and a writing room. Conduct yourself as you would in any restaurant or club. This is your club.

Facilities exist on most stations for practically all games, and airmen are encouraged to make use of these facilities as often as possible.

Have one object always in view: to make yourself the best airman in the hut.

GOOD LUCK, and a safe return as soon as possible to your ordinary life.

**. . . and Impressments** In addition to the aircraft produced for the RAF, 1,017 of the 1,740 civil aircraft registered in Britain in 1939 were impressed into RAF service in 1939–42, mainly for communications duties, and over a hundred gliders were similarly requisitioned for training. Overseas, in the Middle East and India, a similar number were impressed. As they were of over a hundred different types, spares presented a problem, and many types were declared obsolete in 1944. Thirteen impressed aircraft were destroyed at Lympne during the Battle of Britain.

Typical of impressments, a Piper J–4A Club Coupe of the Wiltshire School of Flying used as a communications aircraft, here seen beneath the wing of a Halifax.

Over a hundred Tiger Moths were impressed in India, one of which is shown at Bangladore.

**A Squadron's Name is its Number**   During World War I, the RAF
had used squadron numbers in the Nos 1–168, 185–200, 201–274 range.
Following the disbandment of the great majority of squadrons in 1919,
numbers were re-allotted in the years between the wars.

The great expansion of the RAF in World War II, with new squadrons
forming weekly and the formation of Commonwealth and Allied
squadrons operating under RAF Commands, led to an allocation of
blocks of squadron numbers as follows:

| | | |
|---|---|---|
| 1–299 RAF | 400–445 Canadian | 561–662 RAF Air Observa- |
| 300–309 Polish | 450–467 Australian | tion Post (AOP) |
| 310–315 Czech | 485–490 New Zealand | 663   Polish |
| 316–318 Polish | 500–504 Ex-AAF | 664–666 Canadian (AOP) |
| 320–322 Dutch | 510–539 RAF (Special | 667–679 RAF |
| 326–329 French |    Duties) | 680–684 RAF (PR) |
| 330–334 Norwegian | 540–544 RAF Photo | 691–695 RAF |
| 335–336 Greek | Reconnaissance (PR) | 700–899 Reserved for |
| 340–347 Free French | 547–550 RAF |    Royal Navy |
| 349–350 Belgian | 567–598 RAF | 900–   RAF |
| 351–352 Yugoslav | 600–616 Ex-AAF |    Balloon |
| 353–358 RAF (India) | 617–750 RAF | |

Included in the RAF Squadrons were the three American Eagle
squadrons of mainly American pilots and mainly RAF ground personnel.
These were Nos 71, 121 and 133 Sqns which became respectively the
334th, 335th and 336th Squadrons of the USAAF on 29th September
1942. An anomaly was No 1435 Squadron, the only four digit squadron
number resulting from No 1435 Flight's attaining squadron status in
1942.

The majority of RAF, and an even greater proportion of WAAF,
personnel did not serve in squadrons. They were serving on
Headquarters or Station staffs, Maintenance Units (of which there were
over a hundred in the United Kingdom alone) and hundreds of
miscellaneous units. There were Recruits and Personnel Centres; the
latter for Reception, Transit, Dispersal and, postwar, Resettlement.
Apart from the many schools for aircrew training mentioned later, there
were, to quote but a few, a School of Administration and Accounting at
Hereford, a Battle School at Wombleton, a Chaplains' School at
Cheltenham, a Bomb Disposal School at Doncaster and a School of
Explosives at Tatenhill.

Apart from the flights within a squadron, normally known as A, B, C,
etc according to the number, there were a thousand or so independent
flights numbered in blocks of numbers between 1000 and 9999, for

various duties such as Target Towing, Beam Approach Training, Bomb Disposal, Special Duties, Bombing and Gunnery Training, Radar Calibration, etc.

Not all the units existed at the same time. Units were raised or disbanded to meet operational, administrative or training requirements.

**The Desert Air Force**  While the Battle of Britain was being fought, the RAF in Egypt commenced battle with the Italian colonies in North Africa, Blenheims opening the attack on 11th June 1940, raiding El Adem. Here, General Wavell, C-in-C Army Middle East, visits Air Cdre Raymond Collishaw, who was one of the highest scoring Allied aces of World War I. The aircraft is a Percival Proctor, four-seat communications aircraft, based on the famous Vega Gull, used by the RAF in 1940–55. Below, an Italian hangar wrecked by Collishaw's aircraft in the Western Desert.

**Singapore and the Far East**   Singapore, an island the size and shape of the Isle of Wight, was a Crown Colony. It was connected to the Malayan mainland by a causeway, but its whole defence was directed to seaward with the RAF element composed only of reconnaissance flying boats and strike torpedo-bombers to deal with a threat from the sea. When war came in 1939, No 230 Sqn was directed to Ceylon to widen the search area for possible German merchant raiders. Reinforcements for Singapore included Blenheims from Britain, and Australian and New Zealand units operating American aircraft – Catalina flying boats and Buffalo fighters – but the Vildebeest (example of No 100 Sqn above over Singapore City) remained the only strike aircraft. Airfields were opened up-country in Malaya but these were quickly over-run by the Japanese as they swept down through south-east Asia. Hurried reinforcements, including fifty-one Hurricanes, arrived too late to alter the course of events. By 9th February 1942 only eight Hurricanes remained to engage the Japanese raiders, and these were withdrawn to join other surviving aircraft in the Netherlands East Indies. To spare the large Chinese, Malay and Tamil civil population, the Island capitulated on 15th February. At Hong Kong, whence some Vildebeests had been detached, the capitulation had come on Christmas Day 1941.

Singapore 1938

36 Sqn 12 Vildebeests
100 Sqn 12 Vildebeests
205 Sqn 6 Singapore III
230 Sqn 6 Singapore III
converting to Sunderland

Based at Seletar but by 1941 airfields were built as shown left.

The outposts of Empire were last to be modernized. The first
Blenheim, contrasting here with the Wapitis of No 60 Sqn in India was
borrowed for trials from Iraq. Leaving Habbaniya on 29th December
1938, the Blenheim reached Ambala on 3rd January 1939 where a dual
control set was fitted to train No 60 Sqn pilots who were flying Wapitis.

In the Far East, at Singapore, a 250-lb bomb is loaded on a
Southampton III from an eighteen-foot bomb-loading dinghy, on 9th
November 1936, for air exercises.

Airspeed Oxford, the standard twin-engined trainer of the war and immediate postwar years. A feature of all wartime trainers was their yellow undersurfaces.

**Flying Training, World War II**   Before the war an RAF pilot received 146 flying hours before joining a squadron for continuation training. But in time of war operational squadrons had little time or opportunity for training, and the Group Pool, later named Operational Training Unit, stage was introduced by operational commands before a pilot reached a squadron in that Command. By mid-1941 the sequence was:

### Flying Training

| Training Unit | Duration | Flying | Aircraft |
|---|---|---|---|
| Initial Training Wing | 8 weeks | Nil | None |
| Elementary Flying Training School | 10 weeks | 50 hrs | Tiger Moth, Magister |
| Service Flying Training School | 16–12 weeks | 110 hrs | Master, Oxford, Harvard |
| Operational Training Unit | 4–6 weeks | 40 hrs | Operational types |

An analysis of the number of aircraft written off per ten thousand training hours at each stage showed EFTS $2\frac{1}{2}$, SFTS 5, OTU ten in summer and fifteen in winter. This indicated that flying skill did not increase commensurate with the progression to more complicated aircraft. The remedy was an increase in training time that could be effected largely by virtue of the Empire Air Training Scheme from which the first trainees reached the UK on 24th November 1940.

Miles Magister, first of the RAF's monoplane trainers, which served 1937–49.

**Training Sequence**  A typical sequence of training in 1944 before reaching a Lancaster squadron was

| Training Unit | Duration | Flying | Aircraft |
|---|---|---|---|
| Aircrew Reception Centre | 9 weeks⎫ | 12 hrs | Tiger Moth (local |
| Initial Training Wing | 8 weeks⎭ | | field for aptitude grading) |
| Aircrew Despatch Centre | Variable | Nil | (Awaiting ship) |
| Elementary Flying Training School | 10 weeks | 60–80 hrs | Tiger Moth, Finch, Cornell, Magister, |
| Service Flying Training School | 20 weeks | 155 hrs | Harvard, Anson, etc |
| Personnel Despatch Centre | Variable | Nil | (Awaiting ship) |
| Personnel Reception Centre | 10 weeks | Nil | (Officer and NCO courses) |
| (Pilot) Advanced Flying Unit | 8 weeks | 80 hrs | Oxford, Anson, Harvard |
| Operational Training Unit | 8–12 weeks | 80 hrs | Operational aircraft |
| Heavy Conversion Unit | 6 weeks | 40 hrs | Multi-engined |
| Lancaster Finishing School | 2 weeks | 12 hrs | Lancaster |

Intermediate trainer between basic flying and operational fighters, the Miles Master served from 1939. The 3301 built were in three versions – MkI (Kestrel-engined as illustrated) and MkIII (Wasp-engined) withdrawn mid-1945, and MkII (Mercury-engined) withdrawn November 1950.

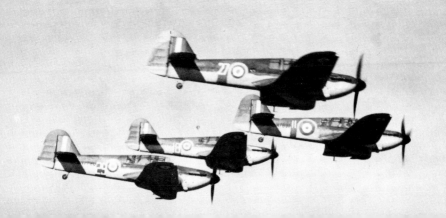

**Armament, Armourers and Gunners** Introduced in 1940, the 20-mm Hispano became the standard offensive weapon in fighters and was later replacing the ·303 Brownings in defensive armament, although the heavier calibre ·5 American machine-guns also came into use. The 20-mm cannon brought changes in aircraft nomenclature – the "armament suffix letter"; eg the Spitfire V with the original 8 × ·303-inch Brownings became retrospectively the VA, those with 2 × 20-mm Hispano cannons became the VB and those with a universal wing, permitting 4 × 20-mm cannon or 2 × 20-mm cannon plus 4 × ·303-inch machine-guns, the VC.

Much was hoped of the Boulton Paul four-gun turret of the Defiant two-seat fighter which first served with No 264 Sqn in December 1939 and had initial success in early engagements in May 1940, but the squadron had crippling losses in the Battle of Britain. As a night fighter, 1940–41, the Defiant was used by thirteen squadrons, and later they formed part equipment of target-towing and air sea rescue units. Mks I and & II were declared obsolete in July 1944 and the remainder (Mk IIIs) in May 1945.

The Battle of the Atlantic was entering a critical stage, and sinking U-boats became Coastal Command's main concern. On 29th November 1941, using new ASV radar, a Whitley of No 502 Sqn was the first Command aircraft to sink a U-boat unaided by other forces. Here, at Oban, a Catalina flying boat is seen being armed with depth charges from a bomb scow.

A Polish airgunner of the RAF explains the working of a Wellington's Frazer Nash turret. Not until January 1939 did air gunner become a full-time occupation. From that time air gunners (except on flying boat squadrons) were also trained as wireless operators and became WOP/AGs. The gunners winged 'G' was introduced on 21 December 1939; previously a winged bullet was worn on the sleeve. From November 1939 air gunners could be commissioned, but the quota was only 13% to the navigators 41%.

**Bombs and Torpedoes**    Bombing up in Britain. A 2,000–lb armour-piercing bomb for a Wellington of No 149 Sqn at Mildenhall.

500-lb armour-piercing delayed-action bombs being prepared in the Western Desert.

Bristol Beaufort, the RAF's first monoplane torpedo-bomber equipped
Nos 22, 42 and 217 Sqns in the UK 1940–42 with limited success as a
torpedo-bomber, but with many operational sorties on mine-laying and
attacking shipping and coastal targets; later moving to the Middle East
to operate from Malta and North Africa, leaving those remaining in
Britain to equip training units.

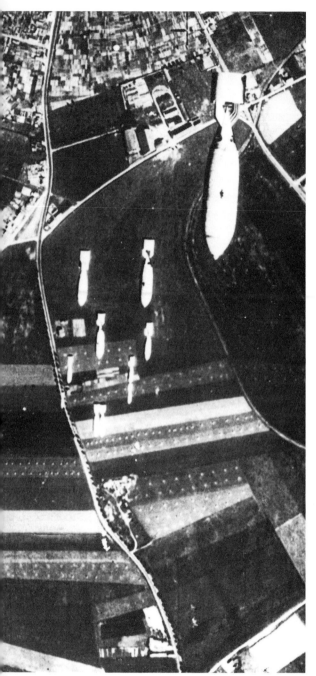

## Circus, Rodeo, Roadstead and Rhubarb

**Operations** RAF Bomber, Fighter and Coastal Commands made constant forays over enemy-occupied territory during 1941 and the years leading up to the invasion of the Continent. There were "Rodeo" fighter sweeps to entice the Luftwaffe to battle, "Circus" operations of bombers with large fighter escorts, "Roadstead" attacks on shipping, and "Rhubarbs" – small scale harassing operations by fighters making use of cloud cover.

While Stirlings were the first of the heavy night bombers, they also operated by day during 1941, including a daylight attack on Emden in April and on the *Scharnhorst* at La Pallace in July. That month Stirlings started operating in escorted "Circus" operations over France designed to bring the Luftwaffe fighters into action while Germany was embroiled in Russia. Picture shows bombs falling from a Stirling over occupied France.

Blenheims of No 21 Sqn are seen flying low to attack shipping at Rotterdam in daylight during July 1941 and below hits on a warehouse (1) and merchant ship (2) at Cherbourg, 7th July 1941. The "North" arrow and other indications were made on the negatives by assessors.

**Photographic Guide** All Commands were well served by photographic reconnaissance: the coastline from Norway to Southern France was covered regularly for Coastal Command, occupied territory for Fighter and Bomber Commands and all industrial areas of Germany for Bomber Command. Here, on 8th April 1941, a Spitfire of No 3 PRU has laid bare the very centre of Cologne, the road (top) and rail (centre) Rhine bridges, the latter leading into Cologne station and passing the adjacent Cathedral, seen as a cross, which the Spitfire was almost directly above when the pilot had his cameras in motion. Such pictures, made up in a mosaic, formed the basis of target maps for the attacks to come and provided Intelligence with an up-to-date view of the growth of German industry. Here photographic interpreters have annotated items of interest for scrutiny under magnification.

**Photographic Evidence**    Another prime purpose of photographic reconnaissance, and a more dangerous mission to perform because it was expected, was the evidence to assess the damage caused by a raid. A PR sortie was flown over Bremen docks, town and Focke Wulf works on 18th March 1941 by No 3 PRU following an attack the previous night when fifty bombers attacked the area dropping fifty tons of high explosive and two thousand incendiary bombs. This is one of many photos taken that day by a Spitfire, and photo interpreters had annotated the photos with numbers to which they made various assessments, including Point 5 showing two direct hits on the railway bottle-neck.

**Malta – George Cross Island** No territory suffered more intensive bombing than the island of Malta, yet it was maintained as an offensive base for shipping strikes and reconnaissance over southern Italy while air defences were maintained at times by fighters flown off from carriers. Left: a local transport commandeered by the RAF is destroyed by bombing.

A Sunderland, right, after a low level cannon-fire attack by Me109s. The most intensive period was May to December 1942 when Malta-based aircraft flew 8,218 defensive, 372 escort, 1,580 reconnaissance, 1,446 shipping protection and 529 ground attack and shipping strike sorties.

It says much for RAF *sangfroid* that the scene below is the AHQ Malta WO and Sergeants Mess re-opening, 20th July 1942!

**Designed to Escort** The Westland Whirlwind (above), designed as an escort fighter, entered service from mid-1940. With too short a range for its intended role, production was cut to 114, and the aircraft joined in the intensive fighter-bomber operations over France and the Low Countries, equipping two squadrons, Nos 137 and 263, coded SF and HE respectively. The Whirlwind was declared obsolete in June 1944. Apart from land-based convoy protection patrols, thirty-five merchant ships were fitted to catapult Hurricanes, manned by RAF or Fleet Air Arm personnel for convoy protection. Hurricanes, below, are being ferried to a merchant ship by lighter.

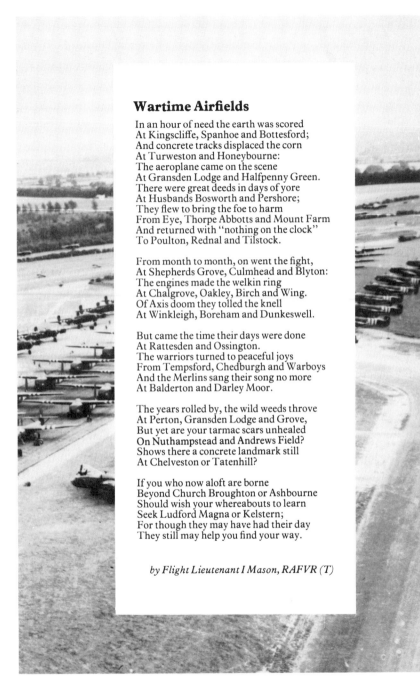

# Wartime Airfields

In an hour of need the earth was scored
At Kingscliffe, Spanhoe and Bottesford;
And concrete tracks displaced the corn
At Turweston and Honeybourne:
The aeroplane came on the scene
At Gransden Lodge and Halfpenny Green.
There were great deeds in days of yore
At Husbands Bosworth and Pershore;
They flew to bring the foe to harm
From Eye, Thorpe Abbotts and Mount Farm
And returned with "nothing on the clock"
To Poulton, Rednal and Tilstock.

From month to month, on went the fight,
At Shepherds Grove, Culmhead and Blyton:
The engines made the welkin ring
At Chalgrove, Oakley, Birch and Wing.
Of Axis doom they tolled the knell
At Winkleigh, Boreham and Dunkeswell.

But came the time their days were done
At Rattesden and Ossington.
The warriors turned to peaceful joys
From Tempsford, Chedburgh and Warboys
And the Merlins sang their song no more
At Balderton and Darley Moor.

The years rolled by, the wild weeds throve
At Perton, Gransden Lodge and Grove,
But yet are your tarmac scars unhealed
On Nuthampstead and Andrews Field?
Shows there a concrete landmark still
At Chelveston or Tatenhill?

If you who now aloft are borne
Beyond Church Broughton or Ashbourne
Should wish your whereabouts to learn
Seek Ludford Magna or Kelstern;
For though they may have had their day
They still may help you find your way.

*by Flight Lieutenant I Mason, RAFVR (T)*

**Airfield Construction**   Some idea of the massive wartime expansion of the RAF can be gauged from the fact that 444 airfields with runways (mainly for the RAF, but including USAAF and FAA) were built 1939–45, employing sixty thousand men at a peak, who completed, on average, an airfield every three days. Apart from runways, there were hardstandings for dispersal with interconnecting lanes to perimeter tracks looking like series of "frying pans" (some here seen occupied by Bostons of No 107 Sqn). Runways increased in size as the war progressed. In 1942 a standard Bomber Command airfield had a 2000 × 50-yard main runway on a NE/SW axis and two others 1400 × 50-yards. Perimeter tracks were 50-feet wide with no buildings within 150-feet of the centre line. In addition trees and other obstructions had to be cleared for some distance at each end of the runways. And for each new airfield, there was a large building-programme of hangars, servicing buildings and accommodation.

# Victoria Cross Awards to the RAF

*"It is ordained that the Cross shall only be awarded for most conspicuous bravery or some daring or pre-eminent act of valour or self-sacrifice or extreme devotion to duty in the presence of the enemy."*

To avoid any duplication in subsequent books on other Services, this list of awards is limited to Victoria Crosses awarded to personnel while serving in the RAF or under an RAF Command. Date given is date of deed that warranted the decoration, except where the award was for more than one deed, or for a period of service, in which case the date of award is given qualified with an asterisk.

### Victoria Cross Awards

| | |
|---|---|
| 2nd April 1918* | Major J. T. B. McCudden DSO, MC, MM. |
| 10th August 1918 | Captain F. M. F. West MC, flying AWFK8 of No 8 Sqn. |
| 27th October 1918 | Major W. G. Barker DSO, MC, in Snipe E8102. |
| 30th November 1918* | Capt. A. W. Beauchamp-Proctor DSO, MC, DFC. |
| 18th July 1919* | Major E. Mannock DSO, MC, of No 85 Sqn. |
| 12th May 1940 | Flg Off D. E. Garland and Sgt T. Gray. |
| 12th August 1940 | Flt Lt R. A. B. Learoyd, piloting Hampden P4403 of No 49 Sqn. |
| 16th August 1940 | Flt Lt J. B. Nicolson, flying Hurricane I P3576 of No 249 Sqn. |
| 15th September 1940 | Sgt J. Hannah, rear gunner of Hampden P1355 of No 82 Sqn. |
| 6th April 1941 | Flg Off K. Campbell, piloting Beaufort I N1016 of No 22 Sqn. |
| 4th July 1941 | Wg Cdr H. I. Edwards, leading attack in Blenheim IV V6028, No 105 Sqn. |
| 7th July 1941 | Sgt J. A. Ward, 2nd pilot of Wellington IC L7818 of No 75 (NZ) Sqn. |
| 9th December 1941 | Flt Lt A. S. K. Scarf, piloting Blenheim of No 62 Sqn in Malaya. |
| 17th April 1942 | Sqn Ldr J. D. Nettleton, leading Augsburg raid in Lancaster I R5508. |
| 30th May 1942 | Flg Off L. T. Manser, piloting Manchester L7301 of No 50 Sqn. |
| 28th November 1942 | Flt Sgt R. H. Middleton, piloting Stirling I BF372 of No 149 Sqn. |
| 4th December 1942 | Wg Cdr H. G. Malcolm, flying Blenheim V BA825 of No 18 Sqn. |
| 3rd May 1943 | Sqn Ldr L. H. Trent, leading in a Ventura of No 487 (RNZAF) Sqn. |
| 17th May 1943 | Wg Cdr G. P. Gibson, leading dams raid in Lancaster ED932. |
| 11th August 1943 | Flg Off L. A. Trigg, RNZAF Liberator of No 200 Sqn. |
| 12th August 1943 | Flt Sgt A L. Aaron, Stirling III, EF452 of No 218 Sqn. |
| 3rd November 1943 | Flt Lt W. Reid, pilot of Lancaster III LM360 of No 61 Sqn. |
| 30th March 1944 | Plt Off C. J. Barton, piloting Halifax III LK797, No 578 Sqn. |
| 26th April 1944 | Wt Off N. C. Jackson, flight engineer of Lancaster ME669, 106 Sqn. |
| 12th June 1944 | Plt Off A. C. Mynarski, air gunner in Lancaster X KB726, No 419 (RCAF) Sqn. |
| 17th July 1944 | Flg Off J. A. Cruikshank, pilot of Catalina of No 201 Sqn. |
| 4th August 1944 | Sqn Ldr I. W. Bazalgette, DFC deputy master bomber in Lancaster III ND811. |
| 8th September 1944* | Gp Capt G. L. Cheshire DSO, DFC, completed 100 missions. |
| 19th September 1944 | Flt Lt D. S. A. Lord, piloting Dakota of No 271 Sqn at Arnhem. |
| 23rd March 1944* | Sqn Ldr R. A. M. Palmer, pilot of Lancaster III PB371, No 582 Sqn. |
| 1st January 1945 | Flt Sgt G. Thompson, wireless operator of Lancaster I PD377, No 9 Sqn. |
| 23rd February 1945 | Capt. E. Swales DFC, SAAF, master bomber piloting Lancaster III PB538. |

# Senior Command, 1939–45

| Aircraft Type | Bombing Sorties | Other Sorties | Aircraft Type | Bombing Sorties | Other Sorties |
|---|---|---|---|---|---|
| Battle | 237 | — | Lightning | 9 | — |
| Beaufighter | — | 12 | Lysander | — | 72 |
| Blenheim | 11,332 | 882 | Manchester | 983 | 286 |
| Boston | 1,597 | 12 | Mitchell | 96 | — |
| Fortress | 51 | 1,289 | Mosquito | 28,639 | 11,157 |
| Halifax | 73,312 | 9,461 | Mustang | 6 | — |
| Hampden | 12,893 | 3,648 | Stirling | 11,074 | 7,366 |
| Hudson | - - | 278 | Ventura | 997 | — |
| Lancaster | 148 ↑03 | 7,789 | Wellington | 37,412 | 9,997 |
| Liberator | — | 662 | Whitley | 8,996 | 862 |

Bomber Command made 389,809 sorties in the course of which 10,882 aircraft were lost and 5,572 damaged. Sorties other than bombing included sea-mining, decoy raids, electronic counter-measures, leaflet dropping, etc. In May 1945 the command strength was 3,691 aircraft and 12,238 engines.

As the war progressed, so larger bombs evolved. The first 2,000-lb bomb was dropped by a Coastal Command Beaufort aimed at a German cruiser off Norderney, 7th May 1940; the first 4,000-lb "Cookie" was dropped by a Wellington on Emden, 1st April 1941; the first 8,000-lb by a Halifax on Essen, 10th/11th April 1942 and the first 12,000-lb high capacity bomb by Lancasters of No 617 Sqn on the Dortmund-Ems Canal, 15th/16th September 1943. The first of 854 12,000-lb deep penetration "Tallboy" bombs was dropped by Lancasters on the Saumer Tunnel, 8th/9th June 1944, and the first of the 41 22,000-lb "Grand Slam" bombs (illustrated below) Lancasters delivered was aimed at the Bielefeld Viaduct. The special bombs taken by nineteen Lancasters of No 617 Sqn for their breaching of the Mohne and Eder dams in Germany in May 1943 were mines, designed to be dropped revolving to skip along the surface of the water to the dam face and roll down to explode at its base, causing shock waves to burst the dam walls.

**"One of our Aircraft is Missing"** "For you der Var ist over." A young fighter pilot, shot down over France early in 1941, is taken into military custody. A similar fate befell the crew of Blenheim IV N3589 who landed on the island of Pantelleria by mistake on 13th September 1940 and whose aircraft was given Italian markings as shown.

**Crew composition** A Wellington crew prepare. Until March 1942
bombers carried two pilots, but from that time it was one pilot per
aircraft. The observer was re-named navigator, and a separate air
bomber was introduced. The other crew members were wireless operator
air gunners. With the new four-engined bomber, a seventh crew member
of flight engineer was introduced from March 1941, trained also to land
an aircraft in an emergency. Irrespective of rank, the pilot was the
captain of the aircraft. From 1941 all aircrew held minimum rank of
sergeant, and squadron leader was the highest rank permitted to fly
regularly on operations. A "tour" with an operational squadron
normally lasted for thirty-one operational sorties.

The fate that befell so many. Stirling BF476 of No 15 Sqn shot down
over Denmark. Happily in thise case all the crew escaped serious injury.

**Service Designations**    In June 1942 the Spitfire IX, with its more powerful Merlin engine, started replacing the Mk V Spitfires – the version built in greatest numbers. This gave the RAF a fighter to match the new FW190 introduced by the Luftwaffe. A patrol of IXs of No 611 Sqn is seen above. In February 1942 significant role letters (eg AOP – Air Observation Post, F – fighter, B – bomber, C – Cargo/transport or communications, GR – general reconnaissance, PR – Photographic reconnaissance, T – trainer, TT – Target tug) had been introduced to aircraft designations and are the basis of the present system of RAF service aircraft designations. The new Spitfire Mk IX became the FIX. With Spitfires there was further qualification. Those with clipped wings (stubs in place of rounded wingtips) and engine rated for low flying, became the LFIX. Similarly, a special requirement to deal with high-flying German reconnaissance aircraft led to special high-flying Spitfire variants with extended, almost pointed, wings, as seen below on a Spitfire HFVI. The armament suffixes remained in use.

**The Tempest and the Doodle-bugs**   The Tempest served in Mk II, V and VI versions, but only the Mk V saw World War II service – first with a Tempest Wing in April 1944. The Mk V shown above bears special identity markings to avoid confusion with German Focke Wulf 190s. After using their four 20-mm cannon, rocket projectiles or two 1000-lb bombs on targets in occupied territory, they were switched to defence in the V1 attack, which started on the night of 12th/13th June 1944, being the fastest of the piston-engined fighters in service. They destroyed 638 V1s out of the RAF's bag of 1,771. RAF balloons played their part and were re-deployed to meet the menace – a balloon convoy is seen below. The Tempest VI, a tropicalized Mk V, equipped Nos 6, 8, 213 and 249 Sqns in the Middle East postwar until Vampire FB5s arrived in the late 'forties/early 'fifties. Many Vs were converted postwar for target-towing. The Mk II, with a Centaurus radial engine replacing the in-line Sabre IIs of the V and VI, served in ten squadrons at home, Germany, India and the Far East and was finally withdrawn in January 1955.

**Operation Hydra – Before and After**   On the night of 17th/18th August 1943 the attack on the German Baltic coast experimental station of Peenemunde had far-reaching success in delaying German V-weapons. Of the 597 bombers setting out, 571 attacked and forty were lost. Views show part of this widely dispersed target before and after attack. Two nights earlier, attacking the Dortmund-Ems canal, Bomber Command had introduced 12,000-lb high-capacity bombs by adapting aircraft bomb bays to take three 4,000-lb bombs made into one unit.

**One Night's War Effort by the RAF**    For the first thousand-bomber raid of 30th/31st May 1942 on Cologne, the 1,046 bombers were mainly twin-engined. By 1944, a thousand four-engined bombers, Halifaxes (No 10 Sqn above) and Lancasters (crew preparing below) were involved in operations some nights. For such a night's operation the aircraft required 2,000,000 gallons of petrol, 70,000 gallons of oil, 5,000 gallons of coolant and 15,000,000 litres of oxygen. They carried some 4,500 tons of bombs, ten million rounds of ammunition, 8,000 pints of coffee and 6,000 lbs of food. The work involved 6,000 vehicles, 3,500 bomb trolleys and 30,000 bicycles working at dispersed sites.

**Statistics – Men and Machines**   The RAF reached its peak personnel strength in July 1944, a grand total of 1,011,427 officers and men and 174,406 women. Previously the peak had been at the end of 1918 when 27,333 officers, 263,837 men and some 25,000 women were serving, but by 1921 figures were down to an all-time low of 3,000 officers and 26,500 men. Generally between the wars, strengths averaged around 3,250 officers and 28,000 men, until the expansion of 1936 when strengths rose from 4,300 officers and 45,700 men to 8,687 officers and 109,324 men in 1939.

The run-down after the Second World War was much slower than after the First, due chiefly to the retention of a National Service intake. There were 76,000 officers and 658,500 men 1946–7, decreasing to 22,000 and 213,000 respectively by 1950. Then, due to the effects of the Cold War and the Korean emergency, causing the enforced retention of personnel, strengths rose to a 277,000 peace-time peak, inclusive of officers, men and women. Thereafter, strength figures progressively decreased. At the end of the 'sixties personnel strengths were 19,300 male officers, 800 female officers, 89,700 men and 4,400 women. In the early 'seventies there was judicious pruning, and in the mid-1970s came cuts to bring strengths down to 15,200 officers and 67,400 men, and 4,600 officers and women of the WRAF. Due to the complexity of the modern Air Force, the ratio of officers to men has changed from one to every ten men in 1918 to one officer for every five men in service today.

Equipment strength of 55,469 aircraft on RAF charge was reached in 1945 of which 9,200 were first-line aircraft. The previous peak had been late 1918 when 22,647 aircraft were held. Due to the retention of large wartime stocks, peace-time aircraft strengths were high by present-day standards; there were 700 first-line, 800 training and 1,800 stored aircraft in the mid-'twenties. Replacement by modern types was on a more modest scale in the late 'twenties, and aircraft strengths fell to under 2,000 aircraft. At the beginning of World War II, total aircraft strength rose to over 3,000 and then rapidly increased to its 1945 peak. Post-war a total RAF aircraft strength of 4,510 in 1950 rose to a peace-time peak of 6,338 in 1952, but in 1958 the holding had fallen to below 3,000. From 2,505 aircraft on strength in 1960 there was a decline to barely 2,000 1967 to 1975, and in March 1976 aircraft strength was reported as 1,908.

**Comforting Statistics**   Helped by the public and various voluntary organizations, the RAF Comforts Committee arranged from their HQ at 42 Berkeley Square, London W1, the distribution of 10,164,670 woollen garments, 61,667 dartboards, 18,628 shovehalfpenny boards, 21,067 chess sets, 438 pianos, 27,129 musical instruments, 8,335 gramophones, 611,594 books, 160,044,794 cigarettes and various other items from October 1939 to June 1946.

**Technicalities – Mechanical, Electrical and Electronic**    Technical Training Command was formed on 27th May 1940, to embrace the existing technical training schools, and expanded to meet the complex requirements for 350 different trades. From 32,000 men and women under trade training at the time, figures rose to the RAF peak in October 1941 of 86,907 tradesmen and 7,446 tradeswomen under training.

As the war progressed, so equipment became more complex. Radio counter-measures were introduced from June 1940; airborne interception radar was introduced operationally in Beaufighters from September 1940, and blind-approach equipment was introduced on operational aircraft before the end of that year. In January 1941 the first of many Ground Control Interception (GCI) units was taken over by the RAF from the Telecommunications Research Establishment, which played a large part in the war in the ether. As a measure of this progress in radio engineering, it is represented that in 1939 a Blenheim, with an R1082/T1083 receiving and transmitting set, could achieve a two-way communication with its base and obtain a position "fix" for navigation – but little more. In 1945 a crew of a Lancaster, fitted with the latest electronic equipment, could navigate and obtain an automatic position "fix", be aware of the nature of the territory over which they were flying on the darkest night, be protected by electronic warning of an approaching aircraft, and train its rear guns to an aircraft target beyond the vision of the crew, and home to base, all with inherent instrumentation, apart from the normal two-way communication systems. To mention but a few of the many other technicalities – fire-extinguishers brought into play automatically with temperature rises, dinghies automatically inflated in an emergency ditching, de-icing fluid sprayed on windscreens when necessary, and fuel-tanks had self-sealing properties.

Below, trained men and women service Beaufighters at No 51 Operational Training Unit, Cranfield, *circa* 1943.

**Marine Craft**   With air-sea rescue commitments, flying boat squadrons and training units, signals units on isolated islands, the RAF operated a fleet of a thousand boats during the Second World War for maintenance, aircrew and personnel relief, refuelling and weapon recovery. Views show, top to bottom, the 45-foot Vosper refueller of 1936–46, the 60-foot general service pinnace and a fire-fighting float.

**Mechanical Transport**    More vehicles than aircraft, and of a greater variety of types than aircraft, were operated by the RAF. Vehicle standard finish from August 1941 was khaki green with a disruptive pattern of tarmac green or light green, small RAF roundel, RAF number and coded letters and figures indicative of the Command and unit. Prior to this, vehicles were in overall Air Ministry grey. Squadron moves, invasion exercises, ammunition and store supplies often necessitated travelling in convoy for which vehicles were normally spaced fifty yards apart as a bombing or strafing precaution as shown. A large establishment of vehicles was necessary for refuelling, ammunition supply, crew transit, etc; the largest being the "Queen Marys" for aircraft recovery as seen below.

**Exercise Spartan**   Exercise Spartan, held in February and March 1943, was the largest military exercise ever carried out in the British Isles, and from it many lessons were learned for training-tactics for the invasion of Europe. The RAF was actively involved in army co-operation exercises and simulating air attack. No 140 Sqn, flying photographic reconnaissance Spitfires, had a special task of photographing activities for a critique of field concealment and march discipline. Here the tracks made by the Churchill tanks are a give-away, and the tanks would have been better concealed close in to the hedge. As to the lorries, they were far too bunched and presented an inviting target for strafing. The writing on the photos was made on negatives at the time.

Monument
Radio masts surrounding building
TARGET (the more Westerly Giant Würzburg)

View looking South

**Invasion Preparation**   By mid-1944 the RAF had meticulously photographed, mapped and charted, the continental coastline from Denmark down to Bordeaux, marking every possible fortification, gun emplacement, communication centre, post and barracks. Here on the familiar Cap Blanc Nez, opposite Dover, German radar and wireless targets have been marked, with the memorial of an earlier war making a fine target-locating point. This photograph was taken on 31st July 1943 by a No 168 Sqn Mustang of Target Reference XII/5; the original markings of the photographic interpreters have been left untouched. On 15th November 1943, the Allied Expeditionary Air Force officially came into being, embracing units earmarked for the invasion, and on 11th January 1944, the strategic air offensive, leading up to the assault, was launched. All strategic bombing was placed under the Supreme Commander for support operations from 14th April. As it was, some targets such as XII/5 were cunningly spared complete demolition to allow them to record the faked plan deluding the Germans into believing that the main blow would fall in the area of Calais.

**Lend Lease to the RAF**  From 1938 a British Purchasing Commission placed aircraft contracts in America including Buffalo, Cleveland, Fortress I, Harvard I, Havoc, Hudson, Maryland, Mohawk, Mustang I and II, and Tomahawk types. From 11th March 1941, when the Lease-Lend Bill was passed, thousands of aircraft were loaned to Britain of a wide variety of types including: Airacobra, Argus, Baltimore, Bermuda, Boston (one seen above in action over enemy occupied territory), Catalina, Cornell, Coronado, Dakota, Expeditor, Fortress II and III, Harvard II and III, Hoverfly, Hudson, Kittyhawk, Liberator, Marauder, Mariner, Mustang III and IV, Reliant, Sentinel, Skymaster, Thunderbolt (seen below), Vengeance, Ventura and Vigilant.

To effect flight delivery, range permitting, a Ferry Command was formed on 24th June 1941, taking over ATFERO (Atlantic Ferry Organization) which a month earlier had opened a new Atlantic route direct to West Africa. After a Transport Command formed on 25th March 1943, Ferry Command became No 45 (Atlantic Ferry) Group. In its peak year, 1944, 3827 aircraft were flown out from America and Canada, mainly to the UK, but some direct to the Middle East, South-east Asia and Africa. Also that year, 3,332 aircraft were flight-delivered from the UK to the Middle East, South-East Asia and Africa.

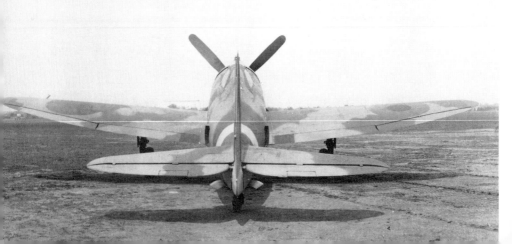

**The Return of the Rocket**    Rockets, used as weapons by both RNAS and RFC in World War I, were re-introduced in 1943 by the RAF in a much more powerful form. They were of three main types: a 25-lb practice type with a solid mild steel head – later of concrete to conserve metal, a 25-lb solid armour-piercing shell of 3·44 inches diameter and a 60-lb semi-armour-piercing shell of 6 inches diameter filled with high explosive. They were fired electrically and a blast plate was normally fitted between the rocket rails and the wing. Here King George VI inspects the rocket installation of a Typhoon which was in quantity production for close support in the coming invasion. Rockets were first used by the RAF on anti-shipping strikes on 22nd June 1943.

The view from the cockpit of a Beaufighter of the Balkan Air Force RAF (formed on 1st June 1944 and disbanded on 2nd February 1945) making a rocket attack on enemy shipping along the Dalmatian coast.

**The Battle of the Atlantic**    A Sunderland flying boat (above, right) leaves the last point of land the crew are likely to see for thirteen hours. The war in the Atlantic fluctuated as the Germans introduced counter-measures for their U-boats, radar-jamming devices, heavier anti-aircraft guns and the Snorkel. The telling measures introduced by Coastal Command were ASV (Air to Surface Vessel) radar which improved throughout the war; Leigh Light for illumination, first used in a night attack on a U-boat by a Wellington of No 172 Sqn 3rd/4th June 1942, followed by the first sinking by aid of the light on 6th July.

The turning point came mid-war, after Allied shipping losses reached their peak in March 1943. Coastal Command then operated over sixty RAF, RAAF, RCAF, FAA and US Navy Squadrons. Twin-engined Hudsons and Whitleys were being replaced by four-engined Liberators and some Fortresses; planned flying and centralized maintenance, now standard RAF practice, was first introduced and more than doubled operational flying hours per unit. In 1918 the RAF had put in hand a programme to replace flying boats with landplanes, then shelved the idea in peacetime but re-introduced the plan twenty-five years later. Among the measures taken was the white finish introduced in the Command in early 1943 for under and side surfaces to render the aircraft less visible from the submariners' point of view, seen below on a Whitley VII which has an array of ASV aerials on the fuselage. The Whitley VII was later used for training in the Command and was, with the Mk V, used for gliding training and paratroop training, being retained until 1945.

Protection over a North African harbour for the invasion of Italy, 1943.

**Anti-submarine Warfare**

*One month of anti-U-boat operations – September 1944*

| Area and Duty | Sorties | Sightings | | Hours flown |
|---|---|---|---|---|
| | | Day | Night | |
| UK Convoy Cover | 51 | 1 | — | 555 |
| Iceland Convoy Cover | 33 | — | — | 309 |
| Gibraltar Area Cover | 35 | — | — | 337 |
| Azores Convoy Cover | 9 | — | — | 102 |
| UK Channel Convoy Screen | 16 | — | — | 55 |
| UK Northern Transit Patrol | 893 | 6 | 3 | 8,382 |
| Iceland anti-U-boat pitch | 59 | — | — | 770 |
| UK Northern Convoy | 949 | 3 | 1 | 7,939 |
| Iceland anti-U-boat Patrol | 17 | — | — | 160 |
| Azores anti-U-boat Patrol | 26 | 2 | 1 | 326 |
| Bay of Biscay UK Patrols | 105 | | 1 | 1,121 |
| Biscay, Gibraltar Patrol | 1 | — | — | 12 |
| Channel Approaches Patrols | 572 | 1 | — | 5,578 |
| Convoy Protection–Gibraltar, Azores and West Africa | 305 | — | — | 2,566 |

Of the nineteen sightings, eight U-boats were attacked, one by four aircraft.

The main maritime patrol aircraft of 1944–5 were the Catalina, Fortress, Halifax, Liberator, Sunderland and Wellington – Liberator GR VIII illustrated.

**Anti-shipping Strikes,
1945** Just one incident in
March 1945 when Coastal
Command anti-shipping forces
had one of their most intensive
periods of operations. Mosquito
squadrons ranged over the
Skagerrak and Kattegat,
Swordfish and Beaufighters
made over two hundred sorties
against midget submarines
operating from the Dutch coast
and Wellingtons did E-boat
shadowing with Beaufighters
making follow-up attacks.
While the Mosquito and
Beaufighter strike wings
attacked shipping, Halifaxes of
Coastal Command made night
attacks on shipping and even
Liberators of the anti-U-boat
squadrons joined in by dropping
depth charges on enemy
shipping as far afield as the
Baltic. Here Beaufighters are
seen delivering rocket attacks
on a convoy escort vessel during
the March attacks.

**RAF Riflemen – Regiment and Servicing Commands**   From 12th
February 1942 the 66,000 RAF personnel employed on airfield defence
were formed into an RAF Regiment. The former defence squadrons Nos
701–850 became Nos 2701–2850 and independent flights were numbered
4001–4336. By 1943 the typical field squadron comprised seven officers
and 178 airmen organized into three rifle flights and a support (with
heavier weapons) armoured car and independent anti-aircraft flights
(operating $12 \times 20$-mm cannon). Later armoured cars were used in the
anti-aircraft role. Five squadrons plus independent flights joined the North
African landings, 8th November 1942, and other units of the Regiment
participated in all subsequent large-scale operations. In spite of a transfer of
forty thousand men to the Army in early 1944 there were seventy-five
Regiment squadrons deployed in Europe in 1945. They shot down the first
jet by ground fire and were first to seize the Focke Wulf offices, capturing
Kurt Tank. Regiment personnel are seen above in Indonesia at the end of
the war.

   It was not only Regiment RAF personnel who were armed: the RAF
introduced Servicing Commandos, of which one unit is seen coming ashore
with their Matador truck in the Sicilian invasion, 10th July 1943.

Jul88s at Gordmoen near Oslo, part of the 579 German aeroplanes surrendered in Norway under ADW survey.

**Operation Eclipse**  Operation Eclipse, affecting a million men and women, was carried out 1945–7 by the RAF tasked with disbanding and disposing of Luftwaffe formations and equipment in areas agreed among the Allies. No 103 Wing formed in Britain in 1944 to train personnel for this task, which took two years by specially formed Air Disarmament Wings (ADWs) operating from May 1945. Their achievements included:

| | |
|---|---:|
| Luftwaffe personnel and auxiliaries (including women) passing through RAF administration | 950,245 |
| Complete aeroplanes disposed of or re-distributed | 4,810 |
| Complete gliders re-distributed | 291 |
| Number of spare engines accounted | 12,800 |
| Barrage balloons disposed of | 51 |
| Mechanical vehicles (prime movers) accounted | 7,064 |
| Marine craft disposed/re-distributed | 334 |
| Tons of bombs and munitions destroyed (Flame throwers and landmines, warheads etc) | 220,000 |
| Rounds of ammunition destroyed | 195,000,000 |

At peak strength, 1,618 officers and 8,005 other ranks of the RAF were involved, plus German civilian helpers; casualties due to premature explosions in loading and stacking munitions at seven different locations were ten killed and nine wounded, all NCOs.

Examining a German A4 rocket (V2) found in a siding; 1,368 V1 flying bombs and 3,002 rockets were destroyed by ADWs.

**Return to the Far East**    Before Singapore was re-occupied by Allied
Forces on 10th September, following the Japanese surrender, RAF photo
reconnaissance aircraft had the island under close surveillance. Here a
Mosquito has snapped the notorious Changi Jail in August 1945 shortly
before its liberation.

The most famous of military transports, the Douglas DC-3 Dakota, entered RAF Service in numbers in 1943, and under Lend Lease 51 Mk Is, 7 Mk IIs, 962 Mk IIIs and 896 Mk IVs were supplied. They acted as glider tugs, paratroop carriers, troop transports, ambulances and freighters in operations in Europe, the Middle and Far East (as illustrated) and were retained in dwindling numbers up to the 'seventies. The first glider crossing of the Atlantic from Dorval to Prestwick was achieved by a Dakota tug on 4th July 1943. On 10th October of that year No 38 (Airborne Forces) Group was formed at Netheravon under Air Vice-Marshal L. N. Hollinghurst in preparation for the invasion of the Continent on the night of 5th-6th July 1944, in which Dakotas played a major glider tug and paratrooping role.

Hong Kong was re-occupied on 30th August 1945, Spitfires of No 80 Sqn are seen at Kai Tak, 29th November 1949.

**Netherlands East Indies**   The RAF were still operational in Java and Sumatra after the war with responsibility for disarming the Japanese and preventing uprisings of factions of the Indonesian peoples. British Forces had a clear charter from the United Nations to maintain order until the Dutch were in a position to administer their former colonies. Supplied by Dakota transports and supported by units in Singapore, the RAF contingent in the NEI, 1946, comprised:

| | |
|---|---|
| Air Headquarters, Batavia | No 31 Sqn (Dakota III/IV) |
| HQ No 904 Wing, Kemajordan | No 60 Sqn (Thunderbolt II) |
| Nos 716 and 721 Met Forecast Centres, | No 81 Sqn (Thunderbolt II) |
| Medan and Kemajordan | No 84 Sqn (Mosquito VI) |
| No 37 Staging Post, Padang | No 155 Sqn (Spitfire XIV) |
| No 49 Staging Post, Palembang | No 656 Sqn (Auster) |
| No 9 Air Casualty Evacuation Unit | NEI Comm Flt (Dakota) |
| Nos 105–106 Embarkation Units | No 2739 Sqn RAF Regiment |
| No 3 Mobile Parachute Servicing Unit | No 2969 Sqn RAF Regiment |

Some of the 830 Thunderbolts delivered to the RAF in South-East Asia, returnable under Lease Lend arrangements at the conclusion of the war, were retained for operations in the Netherlands East Indies (now Indonesia) and are seen here in April 1946 still wearing the distinctive stripes on wings and tail mandatory during the war as identification markings to avoid confusion with Japanese aircraft.

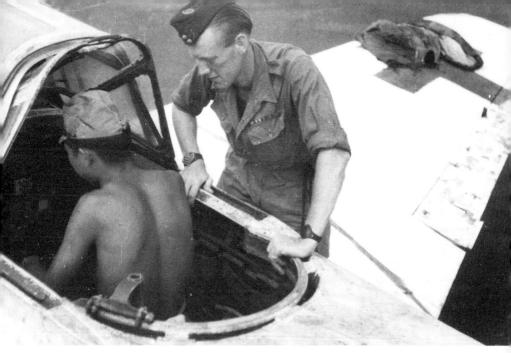

Symbol of surrender. Japanese aircraft required to fly after the acceptance
of surrender on 14th August 1945 were painted white with green crosses.
Here an RAF Flight Sergeant supervises a Japanese mechanic.

After surrender, evaluation. Here Zero fighters, given RAF roundels, are
test-flown by the Anglo-American ATAIU (Allied Technical Air
Intelligence Unit).

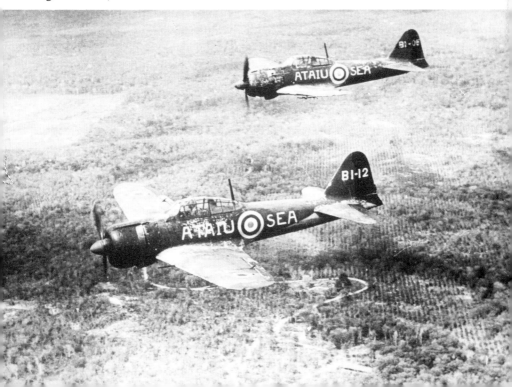

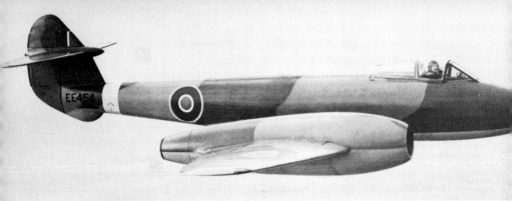

**The Jet Age**   The Meteor, the RAF's first jet aircraft, entered service wit No 616 Sqn at Culmhead, July 1944, making the first sorties later that month from Manston. The first aircraft to fall to a jet were two V1 flying bombs on 4th August, when one was shot down and the other tipped over by the Meteor's wingtip after the guns had jammed. The RAF set up the Wor Speed Record, the first for a jet aircraft, on 7th November 1945, when Gp Capt H. J. Wilson flew Meteor IV EE454 (illustrated) at 606·26 mph. The following year a High Speed Flight was formed with three Meteors EE549–550 and EE548 in reserve, for Gp Capt E. M. Donaldson and Sqr Ldr W. A. Waterman to raise the World Speed Record, which the former did, on 7th September 1946, to 615·78 mph.

No 364365 Boy Whittle, F, became Sir Frank Whittle KBE CB FRS, renowned as the inventor of the jet engine which he researched while serving in the RAF.

**Aries – from Piston to Jet** To investigate navigational problems in 1944, in connection with the switch of Bomber Command operations from Europe to the Pacific Area, Lancaster BI PD328 was fitted out with the latest navigational equipment and left Prestwick on 21st October 1944 for New Zealand via America, returning via Australia, Masirah and Cairo to complete a round-the-world flight. Based at the Empire Air Navigation School (EANS) at Shawbury, PD328 was further modified for flights over the North Geographic and Magnetic Poles which were completed on 26th May 1945. Named *Aries*, this aircraft broke the east-west Atlantic crossing record and later broke the London-Karachi and London-Darwin records. Lancaster *Aries* (seen above) was replaced by Lincoln RE364 as *Aries II* (seen below); this in turn was replaced by Lincoln RE367 as *Aries III*.

The EANS amalgamated with the Empire Air Armament School and the Empire Flying School, on 1st June 1949, to form the RAF Flying College at Manby. Receiving jet aircraft later, the College gave the name *Aries IV* to one of its Canberra B2s (WH699) which broke the London–Cape Town record by flying the 6,009·7 statute miles in 12 hours 21 minutes, averaging 486·6 mph, on 17th December 1953 – the fiftieth anniversary of the Wright brothers' first controlled powered flight. The pilot was Wg Cdr G.G. Petty and the navigators were Sqn Ldrs T P. MacGarry and J. McD. Craig; a new crew took over for the return flight. On 14th October 1954 *Aries IV*, crewed by Wg Cdr A. J. Humphrey, Sqn Ldr D. Bower and Flt Lt F. R. Wood, made the first jet flight over the North Geographic Pole. The following year on 27th-28th June, *Aries IV*, piloted by I. G. Broom, broke the Ottawa-London record, crossing the Atlantic in 6 hours 42 minutes at an average speed of 496·8 mph. A new Canberra, which broke the London-New York and return record on 23rd August 1955, was handed over to the College as *Aires V* – the last of the series.

**Postwar Modes**   Postwar, camouflage gave way to aluminium doping of fabric and natural metal finishes. Another change in the RAF marking came in May 1947. The old wartime roundel and fin flash with reduced white, to avoid compromising camouflage, gave way to a new roundel form. This change is illustrated by a postwar-built Anson C19 cargo and communications aircraft (above) and a Hornet F3 of No 65 Sqn (below). The Hornet evolved from the Mosquito as a long range fighter, and they were the fastest ever piston-engined fighters.

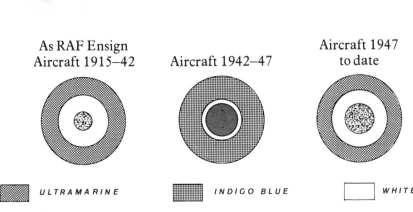

| As RAF Ensign Aircraft 1915–42 | Aircraft 1942–47 | Aircraft 1947 to date |
|---|---|---|

| ULTRAMARINE | INDIGO BLUE | WHITE |
|---|---|---|

| VERMILION | INDIAN RED |
|---|---|

A large yellow outline was used 1937–42 and a thin yellow outline 1942–7 on fuselage roundels.

**The Lincoln Replaces the Lancaster** The Lincoln equipped over twenty squadrons of Bomber Command in the immediate postwar years. It evolved during the war as the Lancaster BIV and BV and went into large-scale production as the Lincoln B1 and B2 to equip Tiger Force for the RAF's participation in the bombing of Japan for which units were moving to the Far East when the war ended. The Lincoln shown is a B2 of No 101 Sqn.

**Transport Command, 1st January 1946**   In the immediate postwar years Transport Command became one of the most important Commands tasked with trooping, repatriation, trunk routing and theatre services.

**Transport Command**

| Aircraft | Units | Base and duty |
|---|---|---|
| 50 Stirling IV | 196, 266 Sqns | UK trunk routes |
| 25 Stirling V | 46 Sqn | UK trunk routes |
| 5 Stirling V | 1588 Flt | SE Asia heavy freighting |
| 5 Stirling V | 1589 Flt | Middle East heavy freighting |
| 60 York CI | 242, 246, 511 Sqns | UK trunk routes |
| 20 York CI | 51 Sqn | Trooping on UK-India run |
| 4 York CI | 1359 Flt | UK based for VIP work |
| 4 Lancastrian | 1359 Flt | UK based for VIP work |
| 75 Halifax III/VII/IX | 295, 296, 297 Sqns | UK based airborne forces |
| 50 Halifax VII/IX | 620, 644 Sqns | Middle East, airborne forces |
| 25 Halifax VII | 298 Sqn | SE Asia airborne forces |
| 175 Liberator CVI/VIII | 53, 59, 86, 102, 206, 220 Sqns | Trooping UK to India (plus 426 (RCAF) Sqn) |
| 20 Liberator | 232 Sqn | } Based in South |
| 5 Skymaster | 232 Sqn | } East Asia |
| 27 Dakota | 24 Sqn | Metropolitan Communications |
| 75 Dakota | 187, 271, 525 Sqns | Trooping UK to India |
| 30 Dakota | 243 Sqn | Australia-Japan routing |
| 25 Dakota | 147 Sqn | Theatre services UK-Europe |
| 100 Dakota | 78, 216, 512, 575 Sqns | Middle East Theatre services |
| 289 Dakota | 10, 31, 48, 52, 62, 76, 77, 96, 194, 267, 353 Sqns | India and SE Asia (48 Sqn disbanded and reformed as 215 Sqn) Includes 19 VIP Dakotas |
| 6 Dakotas | 1680 Flt | UK Theatres services |
| 25 Warwick III | 167 Sqn | UK and Europe theatre services. |

Additionally Dakota units had seven Liberators, two Yorks and three Dominies for VIP and Special Work. Thus the command operated well over a thousand aircraft, far more than the largest airlines of today.

The fatal accident rate was 1·1 per ten million miles on general and 0·65 on scheduled routes, five times better than pre-war airline civil aircraft records.

**Accident Rates**  It would be difficult to analyse overall statistics of accidents in the RAF due to the great differences of Command tasks, particularly of overseas commands, and to judge to what extent operations had a bearing on accidents. The record of Transport Command in training, ferrying and operating worldwide in 1945 provides a reasonable parameter. During 1945 the flying time for the Command rose from 83,000 hours in January to a peak in July of 162,000 hours through additional POW repatriation and transit work, and dropping to 90,000 hours after the Japanese surrender.

*Accident Causes*
*Transport Command 1945*

| | |
|---|---:|
| Pilot error | 286 |
| Landing gear failed | 229 |
| Engine failures | 179 |
| Weather conditions | 179 |
| Taxying | 173 |
| Faulty cockpit drill | 74 |
| MT collisions | 74 |
| Ground crew errors | 63 |
| Airframe failure | 44 |
| Airfield obstructions | 36 |
| Fire in the air | 28 |
| Navigation at fault | 27 |
| Flying control error | 21 |
| Crew indiscipline | 19 |
| Bird strike | 16 |
| Faulty equipment | 10 |
| Aircraft missing | 16 |
| Various and unknown | 71 |

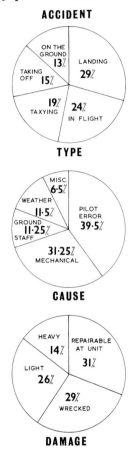

With the unfortunate loss of three aircraft carrying ex-POWs postwar, the Command came under criticism from the Press. However, in an official analysis, the number of fatal accidents per ten million miles was shown to be far less than that of British airlines 1934–8.

**Postwar Re-equipment**    The war brought the need for a new class of aircraft, the operational trainer, of which the Buckmaster was the first example, appearing postwar. At the same time a new identification coding was introduced for non-operational aircraft of black letters on a yellow background with initial letters F, T and R denoting respectively Flying Training, Technical Training and Reserve Commands. The second letter indicated the unit in that Command, in this case on Buckmaster RP246, 'C' for the Empire Flying School (known April 1942 to April 1946 as the Empire Central Flying School). Letters following on the other side of the roundel were for individual identity within the unit.

With a maximum speed of 472 mph at 22,000 feet, the Hornet, developed from the Mosquito, was the RAF's fastest piston-engined aircraft. The 204 delivered to the RAF equipped Nos 19, 41, 64 and 65 Sqns at home and Nos 33, 45 and 80 in the Far East. Hornets first came in service in May 1946 and were discarded in June 1955. In the picture below, Royal Swedish Air Force personnel watch a fitter at work on a propeller of the Merlin 131 engine, during a No 65 Sqn visit to Uppsala, Sweden.

**The Berlin Air Lift**    When Russia blocked the road access to Berlin, and USAAF mounted Operation Plainfare, the Berlin airlift, the RAF, starting from 28th June 1948, used at their peak some forty Yorks, example illustrated, forty Dakotas and fourteen Hastings, supplemented by chartered civil aircraft. The York was Britain's bid to build a wartime transport based on the wings and engine of a Lancaster. The third prototype LV633, named *Ascalon*, was used on overseas tours by King George VI and Winston Churchill.

Hastings, the RAF's new heavy transport arrive to assist on the Berlin Air Lift. The blockade of Berlin was officially raised in mid-May, but the airlift continued to build up stocks in Berlin. During Operation "Plainfare" the RAF made 49,733 flights carrying 281,727 tons of supplies in to Berlin plus 67,373 passengers. The Hastings served for twenty years in the RAF, being phased out in January 1968, but a few were retained for signals work until 1977.

**Restructured Training**   Postwar, all airmen on entry had eight weeks' initial standard training, and trades were divided into groups according to the length of training required, a necessary measure in the early 'fifties when there was compulsory National Service (NS) of eighteen months. 'A' trades of electrician, blacksmith and welder, coppersmith and sheet metal worker, fitters – armourer, engine, airframe and radar, were open to regular service entrants only. 'B' trades of ground and air wireless mechanics, instrument repairers, turners and armourers, of six or more months duration for training, were open to both regulars and the NS entry, as were the 'C' trades of under six months' training, such as technical trades and equipment assistants, clerks and cooks. Additionally, there were boy entrant and administrative apprentices who had eighteen months' training, and aircraft apprentices with three years' training.

Flying training was re-planned with the Percival Prentice as the primary trainer, and by 1950 aircrew trainees went either to Cranwell (128 weeks' course) or to one of three types of school – Flying Training, Air Navigation or Radio, for an average of seventy-five weeks. All progressed to Advanced Flying Schools for ten to twelve week courses and then on to Operational Conversion Units for eight to twenty-two weeks, where they would be joined by engineers and air gunners after their respective seventy-four and sixty-eight weeks' training. Overall, Cranwell-trained pilots and navigators took three years to complete training, and short service pilots, navigators and signallers two years.

The RO (Radio Observer) brevet was introduced in World War II for night fighter radar operators and re-introduced in 1956, after a lapse of thirteen years, for the navigator in all-weather fighters.

The AE (Air Electronics) brevet, introduced in 1956, was applicable to many former Signallers for service in Bomber Command with the V-Force and in Coastal Command on maritime reconnaissance.

The most recent brevet, the QM, was introduced in 1962 to distinguish air quartermasters of passenger and cargo carrying transports. Both men and women NCOs are eligible, thus introducing WRAF as RAF aircrew members.

**FIDO (Fog Intensive Dispersal Operation)**   Fog causing heavy
casualties to returning night bombers led to FIDO's being installed at
Lakenheath, Graveley, Carnaby, Fiskerton, Hartford Bridge,
Melbourne, Bradwell Bay, Ludford Magna, St Eval, Woodbridge and
Manston, 1943–5. Vaporized petrol, burned blow-light fashion, gave
maximum heat with minimum smoke to lift the fog from a runway.
Postwar, an RAF Liaison Party at Manston (members seen in a control
pit) maintained the only FIDO installation in the 'fifties. They kept the
runway on twenty-four-hour standby, 365 days a year, but in spite of
over two thousand wartime FIDO landings – at £44,500 for 250,000
gallons per operational hour – there was only one emergency postwar,
when an Anson in low cloud with an unserviceable radio used the
installation. Experiments were made at Marham in the late 'fifties to use
paraffin instead of petrol, to reduce costs, but progress with electronic
aids made FIDO obsolete in the 'sixties.

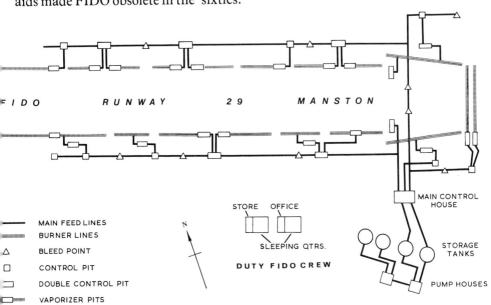

FIDO   RUNWAY   29   MANSTON

MAIN FEED LINES
BURNER LINES
△ BLEED POINT
▢ CONTROL PIT
▭ DOUBLE CONTROL PIT
▭ VAPORIZER PITS

N

STORE   OFFICE

SLEEPING QTRS.

**DUTY FIDO CREW**

MAIN CONTROL
HOUSE

STORAGE
TANKS

PUMP HOUSES

**Re-founding in Youth** To promote and encourage young men to take a practical interest in aviation and fit them to serve their country, the Air Training Corps was constituted on 5th February 1941 by Royal Warrant from the former Air Defence Cadet Corps. Squadrons were formed by school or civic authorities and had affiliations to RAF units. A cadet is seen above in recent years giving effect to the Corps' motto *Venture Adventure* in a Sedbergh TX1 glider with side-by-side dual control seating, after having started training on a Grasshopper T1 primary glider. The part-time training for boys between fourteen and eighteen is normally one or two evenings a week, at some weekends and a camp.

The regular RAF apprentice scheme continued throughout the War. It proved its worth by six thousand former apprentices being commissioned in World War II, with a number reaching Air Rank. Postwar the apprentices at Halton, No 1 School of Technical Training (seen below) and Cosford, Hereford and Locking trained in three main streams – technician (electronic, dental etc), craft (fitters, telegraphists, cooks etc) and administrative (medical, clerical, etc). Some 40% of the entry were ex-ATC cadets. In 1976 the boy entrant scheme ended.

**Reserves – Auxiliary and University**   The flying and balloon
squadrons with former Auxiliary Air Force (AAF) numbers were either
disbanded or re-numbered in 1945. AAF flying squadrons reformed from
mid-1946 with thirteen day fighter, three night fighter and four fighter
bomber squadrons at peak. Their former territorial titles (page 60) were
retained, but some bases differed; eg No 615 Sqn, seen above, flew their
Meteor F8s from Biggin Hill. On 16th December 1947 the "Royal" title
was given to the Force. Nos 661–666 Sqns re-formed in 1949 as Air
Observation Post AAF Units flying Austers and No 622 (Transport) Sqn
re-formed at Blackbushe in 1950 as an AAF unit, but disbanded in 1953.

Ground AAF units postwar included twelve RAF Regiment Light
Anti-Aircraft Squadrons and thirty Fighter Control and Radar
Reporting Units. In 1957 the flying units, equipped with Meteor F8s and
Vampire FB9s, were disbanded and ancillary units were drastically
reduced. Three units remained, Nos 1 (County of Hertford), No 2 (City
of Edinburgh) and No 3 (County of Devon) Maritime Headquarters
Units, responsible for monitoring surface and sub-surface vessels,
manned by men and women auxiliaries. Their training is normally two
evenings per week, one weekend a month, and a fortnight per year.

While the RAuxAF Squadrons flew first-line aircraft, the University
Air Squadrons, continuing the flying club image, flew only primary
trainers as an initiation, starting postwar with Tiger Moths, replaced by
Chipmunks (as shown below) and by Bulldogs in the mid-'seventies.

**WAAF to WRAF**    The Women's Royal Air Force was constituted on 1st April 1918 from the Women's Royal Flying Corps and at peak strength had 25,000 officers and women; it was disbanded on 1st April 1920. On 28th June 1939 the Women's Auxiliary Air Force (WAAF) was formed, with Miss J. Trefusis Forbes the first Director, and they became part of the Armed Forces of the Crown from 10th April 1941. At RAF peak strength in June 1944 there were 174,406 in the WAAF, which reverted to its former title of Women's Royal Air Force (WRAF) on 1st February 1949. WRAF recruits are seen on parade in the late 'forties and manning a control room in the 'fifties.

**The Nursing Service**    The RAF Nursing Service, formed in June 1918, changed its title to Princess Mary's RAF Nursing Service five years later. At that time the Matron-in-Chief controlled five Matrons (allotted to the Air Ministry, RAF Central Hospital Finchley and RAF Hospitals at Halton and Cranwell) four Senior Sisters, twenty-five Sisters and eighty-five Nursing Sisters at home stations and at Aboukir, Baghdad, Basrah and Palestine. From 1944 onwards, the nursing service included airborne work, and below WAAFs are seen handing over a patient to Nursing Sisters for evacuation by Dakota late in World War II. In peacetime the tempo of work has remained high. At Changi, Singapore, at peak in 1968, three hundred general operations were performed each month. At peak in the early seventies, sisters at Cape Zev Ghar hospital, Cyprus, were helping 620 babies into the world each year. The large RAF Hospital at Ely, opened in 1940, admitted 6,000 patients, saw 31,072 outpatients, had 3,385 operations, and 855 babies were born in the wards during 1972 alone.

**Operation Firedog, 1948–60**   During the Malayan Emergency, 1948–60, the RAF were called upon to seek out and destroy Communist terrorist camps and aid the Army in all ways possible, such as by transport and casualty evacuation. RAF operations under the code-name "Firedog", involved 375,849 sorties, by over thirty different basic types of aircraft, flying forty-seven million air miles. Seventy-six RAF personnel and ten RAF Regiment (Malaya) were killed and a total of fifteen wounded in Firedog operations. There were also three RAAF and three RNZAF casualties.

One of the many RAF tasks in the Malayan Emergency was loudhailing, a ploy dating from 1932 when verbal warnings in Kurdish from a Victoria over the Barzan district of Iraq caused the surrender of the rebel Sheikh Ahmed. With a similar requirement in 1953, two Valettas were fitted with external speakers, but the aircraft had too high a noise level and so were replaced by two Dakotas flown from Britain in mid-1954. They operated as a Voice Flight attached successively to Nos 267, 209 and 52 Sqns. Dakota KP277 *Faith* is seen over Malayan jungle with its yellow-painted underslung speakers looking like wheels. For support and salvage work, RAF landing craft were found necessary in the Far East; the initials of No 1 stand for Landing Craft General Purpose.

The RAF took delivery of its first British-built (albeit American-designed) helicopter, the Dragonfly, in 1950 and that same year they were sent to Malaya to form a jungle Casualty Evacuation Flight. One is seen on such a mission (above) rising from a clearing with a casualty pannier carried externally. The flight became No 194 Squadron on 1st February 1953. The Bristol Sycamore, delivered as a rescue helicopter to Coastal Command in 1952, entered service with No 194 Sqn in Malaya in 1954. One is seen below in November 1957 in a jungle clearing at Ula Langut, near Kuala Lumpur, picking up troops of the 22nd Special Air Service Regiment.

**Malaya to Malaysia, 1948–60**   Ten years after the war, the Mosquito finally made its last operational sortie – over Malaya on 15th December 1955, when a PR34 of No 81 Sqn (above) made a final photographic reconnaissance. Postwar successor to the Mosquito, the Hornet, was declared obsolete earlier. Hornets of No 41 Sqn are seen below armed with rockets for a strike against Communist bandits in Malaya.

An RAF Regiment (Malaya) was formed at Kuala Lumpur in 1947, and six squadrons (Nos 91–96) were raised of locally enlisted personnel. They protected RAF stores, sites and installations and undertook periods of jungle duty, killing many terrorists and destroying nearly two hundred of their camps. All but No 94 Squadron was disbanded by 1960 when the Emergency Campaign was over. A detachment is seen at a Regiment camp and operating in Selangor.

**The Coronation Review, 1953**    The great Coronation Review of June 1953 involved around a thousand RAF aircraft. Under meticulous planning by Air Vice-Marshal The Earl of Bandon, over 640 aircraft flew past HM the Queen at RAF Odiham in precisely twenty-seven minutes, having been fed in from airfields all over the country. The review order of this greatest-ever flypast, was:

### The Coronation Review

| No | Type | Station | No | Type | Station |
|----|------|---------|----|------|---------|
| 1 | Sycamore | Blackbushe | 24 | Venom FB4 | Wattisham |
| 16 | Chipmunk T10 | Booker | | (2TAF) | |
| 16 | Chipmunk T10 | South Cerney | 24 | Meteor F8 | Tangmere |
| 12 | Prentice T1 | South Cerney | 24 | Meteor F8 | Biggin Hill |
| 12 | Harvard T2 | Little Rissington | 24 | Meteor F8 | Duxford |
| 12 | Oxford | Wellesbourne | 24 | Meteor F8 | Horsham St Faith |
| | | Mountford | 24 | Meteor F8 | Waterbeach |
| 12 | Anson | Shawbury | 24 | Meteor F8 | Honiley |
| 12 | Balliol | Cottesmore | 24 | Meteor F8 | Wattisham |
| 12 | Varsity | Thorney Island | 24 | Meteor F8 | Wymeswold |
| 6 | Valletta | Colerne | 24 | Meteor F8 | North Weald |
| 3 | Sunderland MR5 | Pembroke Dock | 36 | Meteor NF11 | West Malling |
| 18 | Lincoln B2 | Upwood | 24 | Canberra | Binbrook |
| 18 | Lincoln B2 | Waddington | 24 | Canberra | Scampton & |
| 9 | Lincoln B2 | Hemswell | | | Hemswell |
| 12 | Washington | Marham | 24 | Sabre (2TAF) | Duxford |
| 9 | Shackleton | St Eval | 36 | Sabre (RCAF) | North Luffenham |
| 9 | Shackleton | Aldergrove | 6 | Swift | Boscombe Down |
| 5 | Neptune MR1 | Kinloss | 1 | Victor | Radlett (HP) |
| 3 | Hastings C1 | Lyneham | 1 | Valiant | Wisley (Vickers) |
| 12 | Vampire NF10 | Coltishall | 1 | Vulcan | Woodford (Avro) |
| 12 | Vampire FB5* | Horsham St Faith | 1 | Javelin | Moreton Valence |
| 12 | Vampire FB5 | Oakington | 1 | Hunter | Dunsfold (Hawker |
| 12 | Meteor F4 | Oakington | 1 | Swift | Chilbolton |

* RAAF

The Queen and Prince Philip at the saluting base. In the background are Washington B1 bombers supplied from America under Mutual Aid.

The Coronation fly-past was followed by a march-past of RAF units in Review Order.

**Mutual Defence Aid: the RAF's Share, 1950–58**  Following the inauguration of NATO, the USA approved the Mutual Defence Assistance Program (MDAP) of dollar aid and equipment at the end of 1949. To the RAF this meant new aircraft, ground control approach, airborne electronic equipment and radar search gear.

Coastal Command's MDAP benefit was ex-US Navy P2V-5 Neptunes which equipped Nos 36, 203, 210 and 217 Sqns on maritime reconnaissance, and No 1453 "Vanguard" Flt on airborne early warning duties, from 1952 to 1956–7. An early delivery is depicted. Later some Neptunes were modified in service to have a plexiglass nose and an MAD (magnetic anomaly detecting) tail.

Washingtons, ex-USAF B-29 Superfortresses, filled a gap between the outgoing Lincoln B2s and incoming Canberra B2s in Nos 15, 35, 44, 57, 90, 115 (illustrated), 149 and 207 Sqns in the early 'fifties.

Truly NATO in concept 430 F-86 Sabres, financed by the USA and built in Canada, gave the RAF its first swept wing fighter. To ferry the aircraft across the Atlantic, an RAF Long Range Ferry Unit (later No 147 Sqn) was formed in late 1952 for the aircraft destined for Nos 66 and 92 Sqns of Fighter Command and Nos 3, 4, 20, 26, 67, 71, 93, 112, 130 and 234 Sqns in Germany, where the British Air Forces of Occupation had been re-named 2nd Tactical Air Force on 1st September 1951.

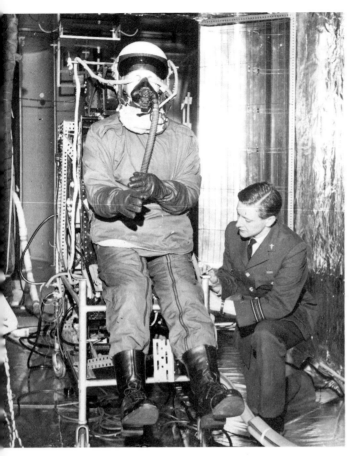

**Service Aviation Medicine** The Institute of Aviation Medicine at Farnborough, working closely with the Human Engineering Division of the Royal Aircraft Establishment, is responsible for research into all factors affecting the operational efficiency of aircrew – heat, cold, fatigue, rapid acceleration, escape methods and survival. At the left a pressure suit is being tested, and below the type of activity that brings human engineering study – rapid deceleration due to safety barriers erected at the end of runways, here seen after bringing a Meteor T7 trainer to a halt.

**Escape and Rescue**    The introduction of the Martin Baker ejection
seat in the 'fifties brought procedures to avoid inadvertent ejection;
above local police receive rescue instructions on a Meteor F8 of No 1 Sqn,
Tangmere, 20th June 1955. The RAF Fire Service, spread over flying
stations, is equipped for all eventualities. Below firemen are being
trained in rescue work on a mock-up Meteor cockpit at North Weald, 2nd
August 1955.

**Experiment, Train and Exercise**   Below, a unit with every aircraft different, the Armament and Instrument Experimental Unit formed in May 1950 by a merger of units formed in 1946 – the Bomb Ballistics and Blind Landing Experimental Units. RAF aircrew worked in conjunction with scientists conducting ballistic research and blind flying investigations at Martlesham Heath, home of the RAF's Testing Squadron back in 1918. Top to bottom: Lincoln with composite jet/piston engines, Varsity T1, Devon C1, Meteor NF11 and Meteor FR9. The unit became absorbed into the Aircraft and Armament Experimental Establishment, Boscombe Down.

Aircraft of the 'fifties represented by the Central Flying School (CFS) in 1954; Sabre, Venom and Hunter fighters leading Canberra bomber and Meteor night fighter centre and Meteor T7 and Vampire T11 trainers bringing up the rear. CFS reformed postwar at Little Rissington on 7th May 1946 and remained there until 1976 when a move was made to Cranwell. It is the CFS that sets the standards, categorizes flying instructors and trains flying instructors for the RAF, Royal Navy and Army and for some Commonwealth and Allied countries. A helicopter wing of CFS operates from Ternhill.

Air exercises play an important part in keeping up operational efficiency and are held at periods to test new techniques and organizations. Here, on 26th April 1955, during Exercise Sky High involving two hundred Canberras in mock bombing attacks and live attacks on ranges in Britain and Germany, Meteor F8 pilots of No 63 Sqn at Waterbeach are seen scrambling for their aircraft.

**Signals and Flying Control**   While barrack blocks and hangars
remain much as built under the pre-World War II expansion scheme,
flying control towers have radically changed postwar. The flat-topped
two-storey towers of the 'thirties, and wartime towers with smaller
windows to facilitate blacking-out, have been remodelled with large
glass-topped structures for local control. Flying control has become
complicated by the increase in civil flying, and in the 'sixties a Military
Air Traffic Operations was set up with close liaison with civil authorities.

Control tower RAF Wattisham in the 'fifties, typical of many such
structures, with GPO facilities, transformer room, air-conditioning
plant and toilets on the ground floor, flight information, teleprinters etc
on the first floor, and controllers, usually ex-General Duties officers, and
their instruments in the glass-sided structure.

Communications had developed rapidly, and No 90 (Signals) Group was
raised to Signals Command status on 3rd November 1958. But with
economies to effect later, it was relegated to No 90 Group and placed
within Strike Command from 1st January 1969.

**Battle of Britain "At Home" Days**   In celebration of the fifth anniversary of the Battle of Britain, it was decided to open a number of RAF stations to the public in September 1945, so setting a style for the years to come. Drastic cuts in the 'sixties (fifty-three stations closed in the years 1961–63 and a further fourteen in 1964) and further cuts in the 'seventies had their effects. In the past four years only a half-dozen stations have been open, in contrast to the past:

Year and Number of RAF Stations open on Battle of Britain Saturday:

| | | | | | | | | | |
|---|---|---|---|---|---|---|---|---|---|
| 1945 | 93 | 1952 | 76 | 1959 | 31 | 1966 | 8 | 1973 | 7 |
| 1946 | 64 | 1953 | 70 | 1960 | 25 | 1967 | 9 | 1974 | 4 |
| 1947 | 75 | 1954 | 57 | 1961 | 16 | 1968 | 8 | 1975 | 4 |
| 1948 | 82 | 1955 | 46 | 1962 | 16 | 1969 | 7 | 1976 | 4 |
| 1949 | 82 | 1956 | 45 | 1963 | 15 | 1970 | 7 | 1977 | 2 |
| 1950 | 71 | 1957 | 37 | 1964 | 12 | 1971 | 7 | | |
| 1951 | 65 | 1958 | 35 | 1965 | 12 | 1972 | 7 | | |

While weather is an important factor in the public's attendance, numbers have increased in spite of the smaller number of stations open.

All heading to swell the growing numbers of cars seen in the park in the background, for a Battle of Britain Day Open Day in the 'fifties. In 1963 it was estimated that 190,000 people visited the station.

**Kenya and Korea** The Mau Mau atrocities in Kenya in 1953 called for punitive action in support of Kenya Police, whose Reserve Air Wing, using Piper Pacers, marked with smoke grenades Mau Mau hide-outs in the jungle. From April 1953, No 1340 Flight RAF used Harvards to drop 21,936 20 lb bombs on hide-outs. From the following October, Lincolns of Nos 49, 100, 61 and 214 Sqns were stationed in succession at Eastleigh, Nairobi, and made in all 517 sorties dropping 1000- and 500-lb bombs on jungle areas in an attempt to frighten the Mau Mau into the open. A Lincoln of No 61 Sqn is seen over Mt Kenya district.

Sunderland's guns manned again. During the Korean War the Far East Flying Boat Wing, with headquarters at Seletar, Singapore, sent out the Sunderlands of Nos 88, 205 and 209 Sqns as reconnaissance and weather flights, anti-shipping and submarine patrols, from stations at Hong Kong and Iwakuni, Japan. From late 1950, the RAF flew British troops to Japan for operations in Korea.

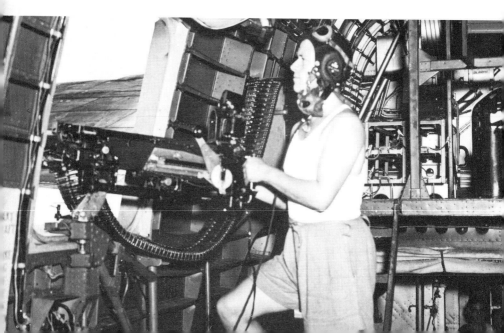

**Swift Saga**    The first service Supermarine jet, the Swift, failed to live up to its famous predecessor, the Spitfire. The Swift F1 with two 30-mm Aden guns (seen above being collected by pilots of No 56 Sqn at Chilbolton in August 1954) was followed by the F2 with four Adens, but both versions only went into limited production. The F3 introduced engine reheat, and the F4, with variable incidence tailplane, proved unstable at altitude, so the Swift was produced mainly in its FR5 (below) version for low-level reconnaissance, being used by Nos 2 and 79 Sqns in Germany. The PR6 version was abandoned, and a few F7s, modified to carry Blue Sky radar and Radar Ranging Mk 2 with a longer nose and extensive internal modifications, were used only for trials.

**Operation Grapple – Nuclear Tests**    Before Britain went ahead with the production of nuclear weapons, after a period of development in the early postwar years, there had to be a period of testing that involved planning and co-operation with Australia in using their own Maralinga range, their off-shore Monte Bello Islands, and remote Christmas Island. The air dropping of an atomic bomb on the Maralinga range on 11th October 1956, and an H-bomb in the Christmas Island area on 15th May 1957, was by Valiants of No 49 Sqn. Further tests were made from the Monte Bello Islands until 1958. During this time some thirteen hundred RAF personnel were deployed in Australasia. The dropping areas had been reconnoitred by Shackletons of No 240 Sqn, and ten Canberras of Nos 76 and 100 Sqns carried out air sampling tests for fall-out, while transport of men and materials was made by Valettas and Dakotas. Whirlwind helicopters were also deployed from Britain to provide a rescue service. The task force is seen forming up in Britain: Canberra B6 bombers above and Valetta transports below. The Valetta, accommodating thirty-four troops, twenty paratroopers or freight, was introduced in 1948, served in four squadrons at home and RAF Germany, six in the Middle East and three in the Far East, being finally retired in June 1969.

**Operation Musketeer – Action in Egypt**    The 1956 Arab-Israeli conflict led Britain, in conjunction with France, to deliver an ultimatum to halt the fighting in the interests of protecting the Suez Canal as an international waterway. On rejection by Egypt, an air offensive was launched on 31st October to secure the canal area. Shackletons joined in the trooping from the UK to the bases in Cyprus, where Venoms and Hunters operated from Akrotiri and Canberras from Nicosia, and Malta, where Canberras operated from Luqa and Hal Far. Valiants, also based on Luqa, made the first operational sorties by V-bombers, their raids being heralded by warnings to avoid civilian casualties. British and French paratroopers were flown from Cyprus, the former in Hastings and Valettas based at Nicosia, and after securing Gamil airfield at Port Suez, No 48 Squadron RAF Regiment took over its defence. Operations were halted in early November at United Nations' request, and a United Nations Emergency Force took over from 22nd November. Illustrated is a Venom FB4 (above) and a Hunter F5 of No 34 Sqn at Cyprus (below) wearing "Suez Stripes", the special Allied aircraft identification markings used for "Operation Musketeer", on aircraft wings and rear fuselage. The Hunter F5s of Nos 1 and 34, brought in from Tangmere, flew cover sorties but were found unsuitable through limited range.

**The Middle East**   On 1st October 1959 British Forces Arabian
Peninsula was established as an integrated Inter-Services Command, the
first since the end of World War II, but in February 1961 the Command
became Air Forces Middle East, while the former Middle East Air Force
became Near East Air Force. A crisis in the Gulf area in July 1961 caused
the ruler of Kuwait to request British assistance. Within a week Hunter
fighter bombers, seven thousand men and 720 tons of stores had been
moved into the area, and V-bombers were brought at readiness to Malta.
In these operations the Twin Pioneer, which could operate from a 300 ×
36-yard strip, proved its value. The following October-December "Twin
Pins" were participating in the emergency operations "Tana Flood"
during which 6,000,000 lb of food was dropped to Africans stranded by
floods in Kenya and Somalia. In all thirty-one Twin Pioneers were
delivered to the RAF and were operated until the 'seventies; the example
shown is flying over Aden.

**. . . The Far East**    The giant Beverley high capacity transport proved a valuable acquisition to the RAF. In July 1956 one dropped the largest load ever from an aircraft in Britain – 24,000 lb of military equipment suspended on 66-ft parachutes. Here, in 1959, men of 92 Sqn RAF Regiment (Malaya) march away from a Beverley which flew them back to Seletar in Singapore from Butterworth in Malaya, making the largest trooplift ever carried out by a single aircraft of the Far East Air Force. The 350-mile journey with eighty-eight fully equipped troops took just over two hours. Equipping Nos 30, 47 and 53 Sqns at home, No 84 in the Middle East and No 34 in the Far East, the Beverley was finally retired in December 1968.

**. . . and Home**    A scene to be repeated all too frequently in the 'sixties and 'seventies: the lowering of the RAF Ensign for the last time on the closing of a station, in this case at Netheravon on 31st July 1963, where the buildings seen had been a familiar sight to the Services since 1913.

**The Day of the Delta**    The Javelin, the RAF's first delta-winged
fighter, was delivered first to No 46 Sqn (shown) at Odiham in February
1956. As an all-weather fighter, the initial version was designated the
Javelin F(AW)1. Twenty squadrons were to fly Javelins in the next
twelve years, using successive marks to the F(AW)9. Basic armament of
the initial versions was 2 × 30-mm Aden guns.

**Arms and the Man**  Firestreak, an air-to-air missile developed by the de Havilland Propeller Co, came into service on Javelin F(AW)7s in 1958. Guided by an infra-red seeker cell in the nose, it locked on to its target before release from the aircraft. The war-head, of 50 lb high explosive, was detonated by a proximity fuse. It is shown fitted to a Javelin of No 23 Sqn.

To celebrate the Fiftieth Anniversary of the first aeroplane flight across the Channel, for which the *Daily Mail*'s proprietor offered a £1,000 prize, the *Daily Mail* sponsored an Arch/Arc (Marble Arch – Arc de Triomphe) Air Race on 22nd July 1959, which was won by an RAF entrant, Sqn Ldr C. G. Maughan, then commanding No 65 Sqn at Duxford. His time was 40 minutes 44 seconds. Picture shows a stage in the race as an RAF competitor, having ridden an RAF motorcycle from Marble Arch to Chelsea, was taken by Sycamore to Biggin Hill for transfer to a Hunter T7 flying the next stage to Villacoublay near Paris.

**Canberra – Record Breaker**   The RAF's first jet bomber, the English Electric Canberra, entered service in May 1951 in its B2 version. Subsequent PR3, T4, B6, PR7 B(I)8 and PR9 versions followed in quick succession from four factories. It first replaced the Lincoln in Bomber Command squadrons in the 'fifties, epitomized by the picture above. As the V-bomber force built up at home in the 'sixties, so the Canberra equipped overseas squadrons. Earlier marks were refurbished and given a new lease of life, and the type continued in training and photo reconnaissance roles in the late 'seventies. Canberras have achieved many world time/distance records, as related earlier under *Aries*.

To New Zealand in a day. Refuelling in the Cocos Islands by a Canberra of the RAF's Race Flight entered in the Speed Section of the London–New Zealand Air Race, 8th–10th October 1953. It was won by No 3 (WE136) Flt Lts R. L. E. Burton and D. H. Gannon who flew the 12,270 miles in 23 hours 51 minutes elapsed time (22 hours 25 minutes airborne), staging at Shaibah, Karachi, Negombo, Cocos Islands and Perth. Wg Cdr L. M. Hodges, commanding the flight, set up a London–Colombo record flight of 10 hours 25 minutes.

**Lightning – Mach 2 Fighter**    Product of the English Electric
Company, later absorbed in the British Aircraft Corporation, the
Lightning supersonic single-seat jet interceptor first entered service in
July 1960 with No 74 (Tiger) Sqn at Coltishall. Capable of over Mach 2,
it doubled the speed of fighters of its day such as the Hunter. With
sophisticated radar mounted as the centre body of the nose, it could track
and engage targets, invisible to the pilot, by Firestreak air-to-air missiles.
The initial F1 version was followed by the F2 which in Nos 19 and 92
Sqns served in RAF Germany from 1965 to 1976. The F3, with increased
power and armed with Red Top missiles, became, with the longer ranged
F6, the backbone of Fighter Command in the 'sixties. To train Lightning
pilots at No 226 Operational Conversion Unit, Coltishall, the two-seat
trainer T4 and later T5, matching the later fighter marks, were
introduced and these aircraft were also issued to squadrons. Squadrons
have been based in Cyprus and Singapore, but the bulk of squadrons that
used Lightnings (Nos 5, 11, 19, 23, 29, 56, 64, 74, 92, 111) served at
home. In the 'sixties, first-line squadrons represented the RAF in display
teams. Nine Lightning F1As of No 74 Sqn formed "The Tigers" for the
1961–2 seasons. In 1963 "The Firebirds" of nine Lightnings of No 56
Sqn took over, making another appearance in 1965. F1As of a display
team are illustrated.

**Whirlwind — Universal Provider**    The Whirlwind, a Westland-built version of the Sikorsky S-55, served the RAF from 1955, and in the late 'seventies was still on communications duties. On 4th November 1961 the Gnome-engined HC10 version entered service in No 225 Sqn of No 38 Group concerned with co-operating with airborne forces, the Whirlwind's task being air-supply, as illustrated (Twin Pioneer CC2s seen on landing strip). From January 1963 Whirlwinds served in RAF Germany and later in the Far East; No 110 Sqn, operating in Borneo supporting Malaysian forces during the Indonesian confrontation, flew 25,000 sorties in five years. They were withdrawn from the Far East in 1967 and transferred to United Nations duties in Cyprus into the late seventies. Called in at times by the civil authorities for uplifting awkward loads, Whirlwinds also performed winter relief work to isolated snow-bound villages in the UK, as seen below, in January 1963.

**Sovereign Bases at Cyprus**　When Cyprus became a republic on 16th August 1960, the RAF bases were restricted to agreed Sovereign Base Areas at Akrotiri and Dhekelia under AOC-in-C Middle East Air Force (MEAF). In February 1961, MEAF was re-named Near East Air Force (Cyprus) and British Forces Arabian Peninsula became simultaneously Air Forces Middle East (Aden). Cyprus remained an important base both in Britain's commitments to North Atlantic Treaty Organization (NATO), with nearby Greece and Turkey NATO member countries, and to the Central Treaty Organization (CENTO). Akrotiri, on the island, became the largest RAF station, and here RAF police are seen patrolling the perimeter on *Atlas* and *Hercules*, the last two horses to be officially on RAF strength; a Canberra is seen at dispersal in background. In the mid-'seventies deployment in the Sovereign Base Areas was reduced following a change in defence policy. Then the clash between Greeks and Turks in 1975 resulted in the RAF's evacuating 13,500 people to Britain by Hercules and Britannias, as well as shuttling between the two Sovereign Base areas, during which one Hercules carried 139 people.

**St Clement Danes**   From the ninth century, there has been a church near Temple Bar in the Strand, London. The fourteenth-century edifice was pulled down and rebuilt by Sir Christopher Wren in 1681, and a steeple was added in 1719. All but the walls and steeple was destroyed by enemy action in 1941. Restored, St Clement Danes was re-dedicated on 19th October 1958 as the Central Church of the RAF. Among the memorials are Books of Remembrance to record the names of 125,000 who made the supreme sacrifice while serving in the RAF.

**Comets 2 and 4**    The RAF formed the world's first jet transport
squadron when de Havilland Comets reached No 216 Sqn in mid-1956.
Two Comet T2 trainers were followed by eight C2 transports. The first
squadron flight, taking the Air Minister to Moscow for Soviet Air Force
Day, was made on 23rd June. One (XK699) flew round the world in
eighty hours flying time in 1959. Five Comet C4s were added in early
1962 – the RAF Mark designations C2 and C4 equating to the civil
designations Comet 2 and 4C. The C2s were withdrawn in 1967 and the
C4s with the disbandment of the squadron nine years later under defence
cuts. Pictures show Comet T2 XK699 *Taurus* above, the first of the
RAF's Comets, and below Comet C4 XR399, the last Comet delivered to
the RAF, seen bearing the shadow of the Hercules from which it was
photographed. Standard finish was white-topped fuselage, otherwise
aircraft grey overall and blue trimmings, and each aircraft had a name.

**Training – Piston to Jet**   The Jet Provost, replacing the Provost (both seen above), introduced jet training to the RAF at No 2 Flying Training School (FTS), Hullavington, in August 1955, when an experimental all-through jet training course started. The first pilot, without any previous experience, went solo on 17th October after $8\frac{1}{2}$ hours flying. From June 1959 the T3 (illustrated) became the standard jet trainer, followed by the more powerful T4 in November 1961 and the pressurized T5 in September 1969. Later the RAF reverted to an initial period on piston-engined Chipmunks, later Bulldogs, before graduating to Jet Provosts.

The Varsity replaced the Wellington T10 crew trainer, entering service at No 201 Advanced Flying School, Swinderby. It served both as a conversion trainer for the heavier aircraft and for crew training. For over a decade Varsitys of No 5 FTS, Oakington, converted pilots for Britannias and Shackletons. In the late 'sixties other Varsitys, with Dominies, trained navigators at Nos 1 and 2 Air Navigation Schools, at Stradishall and Gaydon, but in the 'seventies this training was concentrated at Finningley. In the mid-'seventies Varsitys were phased out; one of the last being illustrated. Their training role was taken over by the Dominie.

**The Years of the Hunter**    The Hunter has a particular place in RAF history, for it was its most widely used fighter in peacetime, over a thousand having been taken on charge from July 1954 in five single-seat fighter versions (F1, F2, F4, F5 and F6). These were followed by the T7 two-seat trainer, the FGA9, which became the principal ground attack fighter in the early 1960s and the FR10 fighter reconnaissance version. Although phased out of squadron service in the 'sixties, two squadrons of FGA9s were re-formed in the 'seventies interim to the introduction of the Jaguar, and in the late 'seventies Hunters are still used for weapon training in their F6 and FGA9 versions. A Hunter F5 of No 41 Sqn is seen above with a surviving Spitfire PR19, and below the famous Hunter aerobatic team the "Black Arrows", provided by No 111 Sqn, is seen taking off. This team used up to five F4s in 1956, seven to nine F6s in 1957 and nine to sixteen F6s in 1958–60. Other named Hunter aerobatic teams were the "Fighting Cocks" and "Black Knights", using four F4s in 1956, provided by Nos 43 and 54 Sqns respectively, and the "Blue Diamonds" of sixteen F6s displayed 1961–2 provided by No 92 Sqn.

**Central and Regional Bands**   When the RAF formed in 1918, Sir
Walford Davies was appointed the first Director of Music and his
successor in 1919, Sir George Dyson, founded the Central Band of the
RAF in April 1920. From 1920 to 1930 Flg Off (later Flt Lt) J. H. Amers
directed, to be followed in sequence by Wing Commanders
R. P. O'Donnell (1931–49), A. E. Sims (1949–60), J. Wallace
(1960–69) and R. E. C. Davies. The Band was maintained throughout
the war, and in 1944 110 bandsmen went on an exchange posting to the
USA. In 1956 the first of the annual RAF Anniversary concerts was held
on 7th April, attended by HM the Queen. At the 1956 concert, with Sir
John Barbirolli and the Hallé Orchestra, Tchaikovsky's 1812 Overture
was played for the first time in this country as the composer intended, by
both band and orchestra. The Central Band is seen at Uxbridge, 24th
May 1973 (above), and the Western Band at the final RAF parade at
Changi, Singapore – Shackleton MR2 of No 205 Sqn, a unit which has
had an association with the island since 1928, in the background.

**Royal Flights**   A King's Flight was formed in 1937 when an Airspeed Envoy III was acquired. During World War II, when the Flight consisted of a DH Flamingo, a Percival Q6 and a Lockheed Hudson, King George VI suggested that the aircraft might be more usefully employed in general communications duties, and the Flight disbanded on 14th February 1942. On later wartime flights the King used the VIP York *Ascalon* and in 1945 Dakota IV KN386. On 1st May 1946 a new King's Flight was reformed under King Edward VIII's former pilot, Air Cdre E. A. Fielden CB CVO DFC AFC. Four Vikings were delivered from August 1946, VL245 the staff aircraft, VL246–7 for the King and Queen respectively and VL248 a workshop version. Princess Elizabeth (later Queen) is seen above arriving at Leuchars, 4th August 1951, in VL246 to present the Esher Trophy. In 1955, after becoming The Queen's Flight, a Heron in Edinburgh Green trim was delivered, followed in 1958 by two Heron C3s in royal blue trim which served for ten years. Current equipment is two Hawker Siddeley Andover CC2s XS789–90, one of which is seen below with a Heron behind. A Dragonfly helicopter was attached to the Flight in the early 'fifties, and two helicopters became permanently on establishment from November 1959, when Westland Whirlwind CC8s XN126 and XN127 were delivered, replaced by Gnome-engined HCC12s in 1964. Currently Westland Wessex HCC4s XV726–7 are used at the Flight's base at RAF Benson.

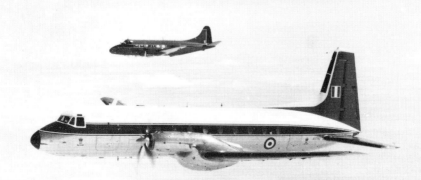

**Missile Age –**

**Thor, . . .**   This was the age of the missile, and the manned aircraft was seen in the 'fifties as rapidly becoming obsolescent, but in spite of missiles deployed in the 'sixties for aerial offence and defence, the manned aircraft is still much in evidence in the 'seventies and planned for the 'eighties.

In August 1958 the first IRBM (Intermediate Range Ballistic Missile) squadron (No 77 of Bomber Command) formed at Feltwell and the first Douglas-built Thor missile was handed over on 19th September. The first trial RAF launching of Thor was in the USA at Vandenberg on 16th April 1959, seen here being prepared. Some sixty were deployed in East Anglia and Yorkshire. This 65-foot missile, weighing 110,000 lb, reached over Mach 10 at burn-out. It was phased out in 1963.

**Bloodhound and Blue Steel**   The Bloodhound area defence missile
entered service in July 1958 operated by Fighter Command squadrons in
units of sixteen, for defence of V-bomber and Thor missile bases. An
improved Mk 2, less susceptible to counter-measures, replaced the Mk 1
in the 'sixties and was deployed in Malaysia from 1964 and in Germany
in the 'seventies. A Bloodhound is shown being brought to its launcher by
a special side-loading fork-lift truck.

Within two days of the ending of the Emergency in Malaya, 31st July
1960, economies were announced. By the introduction of Skybolt and
Blue Steel ballistic missiles, air-launched from Vulcans and Victors, a
nuclear strike deterrent could be maintained with fewer aircraft, and 'V'
bombers orders were cut. As it was, Skybolt was not adopted, and
although Blue Steel (seen being transferred from carrier to cradle for
sliding under a V-bomber) went into service in 1962, the nuclear
deterrent role passed to Royal Navy Polaris-armed submarines.

**Radfan Operations**   The RAF's only twin-rotor helicopter, the Belvedere, entered service with No 66 Sqn at Odiham in September 1961, and the twenty-six delivered served at home, in Aden and the Far East; it was withdrawn from service in March 1969. Here a Belvedere of No 26 Sqn lifts 105-mm howitzers of 'J' Battery, Royal Artillery, during the Radfan operations. These operations resulted from the Dhala Road, one of the main trade routes, being closed by dissident tribes in the mountainous area thirty-five miles north of Aden. The Federation of South Arabia sought British help in forcing the opening of the vital road, leading to RAF action against tribes whom they had fought forty years previously. Apart from the RAF helicopter support, Shackletons of No 37 Sqn gave hours of illumination at night by flares to assist the army, and Hunter FGA9s of Nos 8, 43 and 208 Sqns made strafing sorties with 30-mm cannon and rockets over ground mapped by Hunter FR10s of No 1417 Flt.

**Goodbye to the Gulf**   The last Armstrong Whitworth design for the
RAF was the Argosy. The first of the fifty-six delivered went to Benson in
November 1961 for conversion training, and the aircraft served in the
'sixties at home and in MEAF and FEAF in Nos 70, 105, 114, 115, 215
and 267 Sqns as transports and paratroopers. Each carried a crew of four
and up to sixty-nine troops, fifty-four paratroopers or forty-eight
stretcher cases. They were withdrawn in the mid-'seventies, except for a
few employed on instrument calibration. Those shown are flying along
the coast of Aden. Transport Command, re-named Air Support
Command from 1st August 1968, was given increased responsibility for
long-range strategic and tactical air assault and support roles, but the
spheres of responsibility were contracting. The RAF left the installation
at Aden with the general withdrawal from the Gulf area in 1971,
completed by 21st December, except for the island staging post of
Masirah, retained until 1976.

**Marine Craft for the 'Seventies** With the abandoning of flying boats, many miscellaneous tenders disappeared from the RAF, but from the late 'sixties there was a need for larger support and weapon recovery craft as well as a continuing air-sea rescue role. HMAFV *Seal* (above), launched in 1967, is the first of three (others are *Seagull* and *Sea Otter*) long-range support craft in service, with a top speed of twenty-eight knots and a complement of twenty. HMAFV *Spitfire* (below), with *Sunderland* and *Halifax*, are a new class of craft in the 'seventies for aircrew training co-operation and target towing.

**BMEWS (Ballistic Missile Early Warning System)**    Landmarks at
Fylingdales on the Yorkshire moors, are the great 140-foot-diameter
fibre glass domes (above) covering the radar heads (example below)
which, linked to sensors and computors, provide a surveillance of
airspace in the integrated Anglo-American BMEWS. Operated by the
RAF and constantly on the alert, the high power radars operating in the
ultra-high frequency band have a range of some three thousand miles.
The system also tracks and identifies the various satellites encircling the
earth. Built and equipped at a cost of £45 million, of which the US
Government paid £36 million, Fylingdales is one of three stations, the
other two being at Thule, Greenland, and Clear Air Force Base in
Alaska. The system entered its sustained operational phase from 15th
January 1964. In 1973 spidermen spent seven weeks applying 850
gallons of pale blue paint, plus 200 gallons of thinners, over the three
radomes.

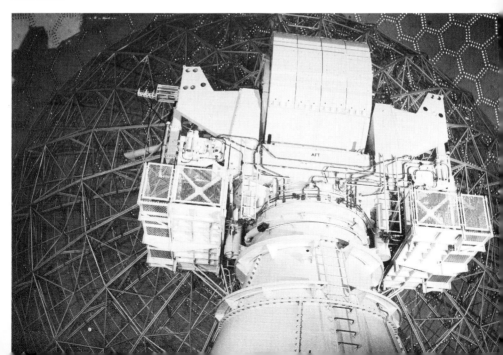

**Short Haul**    Replacing the Anson in the communications role was the Hunting Percival Pembroke; forty-four were acquired, and they entered service late 1953 and were serving in the mid-'seventies in communications squadrons at home and in RAF Germany. The Pembroke C1 had a crew of two and accommodated eight passengers.

Acquired by the RAF in 1965 were twenty Basset CC1s, a version of the civil Beagle B206, for service in the Northern, Metropolitan and Southern Communications Squadrons which became Nos 26, 32 and 207 Sqns respectively in 1969. The Bassets were withdrawn in 1975.

**Long Range**   While not the largest, the BAC VC10 was the heaviest aircraft to enter RAF service. A long-range strategic transport, the VC10 had capacity for 150 passengers or seventy-six stretcher cases and attendants and could fly 3,650 miles before needing refuelling. Delivered to the RAF in April 1966, the fourteen VC10s of No 10 Sqn Air Support Command were named after RAF VCs on Armistice Day 1968. On 31st July 1969 a VC10 landed at Brize Norton having completed a west-about circle of the world in $45\frac{1}{2}$ hours.

The RAF's first turbo-prop transport, the Bristol Britannia entered service in 1959. The twenty-three acquired, operated by Nos 99 and 511 Sqns, provided rapid deployment of the Army's UK Strategic Reserve. They brought relief to Belize when the city was devastated by a hurricane in November 1961, under operation "Sky Help". During 1966 the Britannias were involved, as shown below, in the airlift of $3\frac{1}{2}$ million gallons of fuel to Zambia following Rhodesia's unilateral declaration of independence. Britannias were withdrawn in 1976.

**Confrontation**    After the Malayan Emergency, the new independent Malaysia faced Indonesian confrontation to its territory of Sabah (formerly North Borneo) and Sarawak. The Pioneer (above) with its short take-off and landing capability again came into its own, and British, Gurkha and Malaysian troops were also supplied by Wessex helicopters and by air-drops from Beverleys and Argosys, loading at Labuan, Sabah (where a No 215 Sqn Argosy is seen below being loaded with a one-ton supply container from a fork-lift truck) and from Kuching in Sarawak. The confrontation ended in August 1966.

**Wessex and Puma**    Replacing the Whirlwind in its army support role, the Wessex (Westland-built version of the Sikorsky S-58) HC2 entered service with No 18 Sqn of No 38 Group in February 1964, seen above that year. No 18 Sqn later went to RAF Germany and No 72 Sqn, formerly with Belvederes, became a Wessex Squadron; the helicopters of No 72 were flown to Malaysia in Belfasts for operation "Bersatu Padu" in June 1970. The Wessex, with capacity for sixteen troops, was supplemented by the Westland-built French-designed Puma from late 1970, entering No 33 Sqn of No 38 Group from 29th September 1971. Pumas below, seen being refuelled, have a maximum speed of 174 mph and a range of 275 nautical miles.

**Royal Review**   The Queen, accompanied by Prince Philip, reviews her Air Force from an RAF Land Rover.

**Fiftieth Anniversary, 1968**   The Fiftieth Anniversary of the RAF, 1st April 1968, was celebrated throughout the year, culminating in a Royal Review at Abingdon on 14th June, where a static park and fly-past represented the RAF over the years, followed by a public visiting day and flying display.

**Strike Command**    In the fiftieth year of the RAF came the most
significant changes in organization since 1936. A single main operational
force, Strike Command, was formed by a merger of Fighter and Bomber
Commands. On 1st June Flying Training and Technical Commands
merged into a single Training Command. The rationalization of the
Home Commands from eight to four was completed on 25th November
1969 when Coastal Command became No 18 (Marine) Group of Strike
Command. From 13th June 1977 Training and Support Commands
merged to become Support Command.

A Lancaster, symbolic of Bomber Command, dips in salute over Bentley
Priory, former HQ of Fighter Command, on 30th April 1968, the day
Strike Command formed.

**Command Structure Review**    The Anson, entering the year the functional command organization was introduced (1936), continued in production for navigational and twin-engined flying training during World War II, and new versions were built postwar for communications and training. It served at times in Coastal, Transport, Flying Training, Reserve and Home Commands in quantity and in other Commands in limited numbers. Here, on 28th June 1968, Anson C19 VL349 of Air Support Command makes the last service flight of an RAF Anson.

Over the years Command Structure at home has changed greatly since 1936 when area commands gave way to functional commands, and the various functions expanded during World War II and contracted in the years that followed, as given in charted form below.

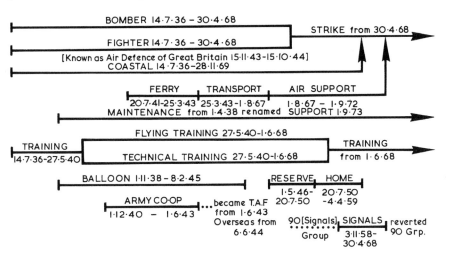

# HOME COMMAND STRUCTURE FROM 14 JULY 1936

## Parachute Training

Parachute training for all three Services is an RAF responsibility. No 1 Parachute Training School in postwar years trained some two thousand parachutists a year for the three Services. Two squadrons at the School trained the Airborne Forces, and a third squadron trained RAF instructors and miscellaneous parties such as RAF Medical Rescue Teams. Training started with ground jumps and then controlled harnessed seventy-foot tower descents. An intermediate stage to drop from aircraft – Dakotas, Hastings, Beverleys, Argosys over the years and currently Hercules – was the 800 foot drop from a "cage" slung from a tethered balloon as shown. The School started as the Central Landing Establishment at Ringway where the bulk of Britain's wartime Airborne Forces were given their parachute training, and from 1950 to early 1970 was at Abingdon; recently it moved to Brize Norton.

**"The Falcons"**   The RAF Free Fall Parachute Display Team "The Falcons" epitomize the motto of the Parachute Training School, "*Knowledge Dispels Fear*". For ten years they have been the premier display team and are capable of landing twelve parachutists within twenty yards of a target after performing a free-fall aerial pattern for one minute after jumping from an aircraft. The parachutes used (right) are the Pioneer Para Commander designed in the early 1960s, which is a form of non-rigid glider giving a still air forward speed of 10–12 mph. They are appropriately coloured red, white and blue in roundel form. All members of the RAF may parachute through the RAF Sport Parachute Association, which operates its own Cessna 206 light aircraft.

**Air Support**   Replacing Beverleys and Hastings as the medium range tactical transports, sixty-six Lockheed Hercules were delivered from late 1966. Apart from their routine supply flights and exercises, Hercules became involved in several emergency missions. During the Indo-Pakistan War in December 1971, Hercules evacuated 909 British and friendly nationals from West Pakistan, and another 434 were snatched to safety by Hercules using a shell-cratered runway in East Pakistan. In March 1973 Hercules, in the largest airlift since Berlin, brought succour to starving Nepalese villagers in the Himalayas in operation "Khana Cascade", dropping two thousand tons of grain, maize and rice, after setting up a base at Bhairawa, seen above during the operation.

A tactical transport, the Hawker Siddeley Andover C1 featured a beaver tail for air-dropping supplies by parachute (as illustrated) and a "kneeling undercarriage" to permit rear loading of vehicles. The first of 31 Andover C1s entered service with No 46 Sqn in July 1966, and they also served in Nos 52 and 84 Sqns in the Far East and the Gulf respectively. The type was withdrawn from squadron service in 1976. Additionally six Andover CC2s, based on the civil HS748, were acquired and are still serving.

**Hangars and Pallets**   Most RAF accommodation dates back to the pre-war expansion period and wartime building, but some new structures were essential postwar. The RAF Technical College moved from Henlow to Cranwell on 3rd January 1966, necessitating a second Officers' Mess, new Sergeants' Mess and Airmen's Club, re-fitting the instructional workshops. On 17th May 1966, Lord Trenchard opened a new Trenchard Hall, which was followed by a new Aerothermodynamics Block opening in June. At Lyneham a new air terminal, capable of handling three hundred passengers at a time, was opened in April 1961, and a new base-servicing hangar (seen above), one of the largest in Europe, was completed at Brize Norton. This hangar could accommodate six VC10s or Belfasts, the latter having entered service in No 53 Sqn late 1966.

A Hercules demonstrates ULLA (Ultra-low-level air-drop) delivery of supplies in a pallet pulled from the aircraft by parachute.

**V-Bombers**    The three V-bombers were all aircraft exclusive to the RAF. The Vickers Valiant, first of these four-jet bombers designed for the nuclear deterrent role, entered service with No 138 Sqn at Gaydon in January 1955, and the 104 built equipped ten squadrons. On 11th October 1956 Valiant VZ366 over the Maralinga range made the first release of a British nuclear bomb, and on 15th May 1957 XD818 dropped the first British H-bomb at Christmas Island. Meanwhile, Valiants had been operational from Malta in the Suez campaign with conventional bombs. Valiants were withdrawn December 1964.

The delta-winged Avro Vulcan entered service with No 230 Operational Conversion Unit (OCU) in May 1958. The forty-five B1s were superseded by the B2 which could carry the Blue Steel stand-off bomb or $21 \times 1000$-lb conventional bombs, and the latter mark became operational in the mid-'sixties as a low-level penetration force. On 9th September 1956, B1 XA897 flew to Melbourne, 11,475 miles in just over twenty-three hours' flying, $47\frac{1}{2}$ hours elapsed time. The first non-stop UK-Australia (11,500 miles) flight was made by a Vulcan on 20th-21st June 1961 in twenty hours', refuelled in Cyprus, Karachi and Singapore.

Third V-bomber, the crescent-winged Handley-Page Victor, entered No 232 OCU from 29th November 1957. The earlier B1s deployed from 1958 in the deterrent role took over the former refuelling duties of the Valiants. The improved B2 and its strategic reconnaissance SR2 Victor versions were both withdrawn, some being modified as Victor K2s to provide a tanker force for the future.

**Flight Refuelling**    Flight refuelling had been a Valiant task from 1958, and forty-five were made tanker aircraft (BK1s). Air-refuelled twice, a Valiant made the first non-stop Cape flight, 6,060 miles in 11·47 hours, on 9th July 1959. Victors took over the tanker role in the mid-'sixties, serving in Nos 55, 57 and 214 Sqns. One is seen below refuelling a Buccaneer and Lightning. When ten Lightnings of No 11 Sqn visited the Far East in January 1969, their 18,500 mile journey entailed 228 contacts to transfer 166,000 gallons of fuel.

**Withdrawal from Singapore** From 1967 onwards, the RAF started to withdraw from east of Suez in accordance with political policy, but with capability rapidly to reinforce by UK-based units. Under Operation "Bersatu Padu" in April/May 1970, Belfast, Britannia, Hercules and Belfast VC10s conveyed 2,265 personnel and $1\frac{1}{2}$ million pounds of equipment, including 350 vehicles and twenty helicopters, in a reinforcing exercise to Singapore for troop deployments in Malaysia. The Far East Air Force disbanded on 1st November 1971, and a small RAF presence was maintained by Shackletons and Whirlwinds, replaced later by Nimrods and Wessex as part of a five-Power defence force; but all were withdrawn in the mid-'seventies. A Vulcan of No 101 Sqn is seen over the Singapore waterfront in 1974 above, and a 103 Sqn Wessex delivers Admiral Sir Terence Lewin to HMS *Lowestoft* off Singapore.

**Presence at Hong Kong**  The main RAF airfield at Hong Kong is Kai Tak, which developed from an RAF station to an international airport with the RAF occupying part. This is at Kowloon on the mainland, as the island itself is too hilly for an airfield. The RAF presence since early 1948 has been provided by No 28 Sqn, first with Spitfires, then successively with Vampires, Venoms and Hunters. No 28 reformed with Wessex helicopters currently used; this picture shows one of these helicopters in the RAF compound, which is hemmed in by the environs of Kowloon. In the foreground is a refurbished Venom FB4, kept as a monument to the days when the squadron flew fighters. The Wessex currently have a support role with the Infantry Brigade stationed in Hong Kong and the New Territories. UK-based fighters such as Phantoms have visited Hong Kong via Singapore on exercises.

**The Queen's Colour Squadron** The Queen's Colour Squadron of the RAF Regiment are the custodians of the Queen's Colour for the RAF in the UK and represent the RAF on most ceremonial occasions. In eighteen years they have given over six hundred continuity drill parades and provided Guards of Honour and representation at a similar number of ceremonial occasions. At the left, a member of the Queen's Colour Squadron is "first relief", taking over from the Guards at Buckingham Palace in October 1974. The Squadron are best known for their complex continuity drill, without word of command, which they are seen performing below at Cardiff Castle in July 1975.

**Service Dogs** The RAF used guard dogs extensively during World War II, but not until 1946 did the RAF Police assume dog training responsibility on the disbandment of the Ministry of Aircraft Production Guard Dog School. In the mid-'seventies some two hundred dogs, mostly Alsatians and some Labradors, were recruited and trained annually to meet a required deployment of some seven hundred dogs for guard, tracking and detection duties. An Alsatian guard-dog and handler are seen at Akrotiri, Cyprus (right), with a Lightning of No 56 Sqn in the background, and (below) a Labrador on anti-sabotage duty, trained to detect explosives, sniffs around the flight deck of a VC10 at Brize Norton in 1973.

## The Mountain Rescue Service

The RAF Mountain Rescue Service can be traced back to April 1942 when Flt Lt G. Graham, station medical officer of RAF Llandwrog, organized search and rescue parties, bringing twelve aircrew to safety by the end of the year. Since 571 Allied airmen had lost their lives in upland area crashes in the UK in 1943 alone, a Mountain Rescue Service was officially established in January 1944. Teams were later introduced overseas, at Cyprus in 1954, Aden in 1960 and Hong Kong in 1961. In the 'seventies there were six teams with from twenty-five to thirty-six members on a voluntary basis, with a regular nucleus of an NCO team leader, two drivers, a wireless operator and storeman. A team member is seen during a recent practice.

**Air – Sea Rescue, at Home and Overseas** The RAF in Britain in the 'sixties and early 'seventies maintained two Air-Sea Rescue squadrons in the UK, equipped with Whirlwinds deployed in flights around the coasts. A Whirlwind is seen above co-operating with an RAF rescue launch. In the mid-'seventies Wessex helicopters started to replace the Whirlwinds in the rescue role, and in the late 'seventies RAF Sea Kings HAS3s are coming into service for this role. Below, a Near East Air Force land-rescue team make ready their air-dropped Land Rover in Cyprus.

**The Queen's Birthday and other Flypasts**   Battle of Britain Day "flypasts" over London were led by a veteran aircraft until September 1959 when Spitfire LF16e SL574 force landed at Downham, SE London, after an engine failure. As a result flights by veteran fighters were no longer permitted over London. After being salvaged, as seen above, SL574 stood guard outside St George's Chapel, Biggin Hill, and later "starred" in the film *Battle of Britain*.

Flypasts at Battle of Britain Day, and to celebrate the Queen's Birthday, are annual events, but the number of aircraft involved have dwindled over the years. Here in a 1973 flypast, Strike Command show representative aircraft, four Vulcans flanked by Buccaneers, Phantoms and two flights of Lightnings.

233

**Phantom and Buccaneer** The McDonnell Douglas Phantom, F-4 of the US Services, entered RAF service from 20th July 1968. The FGR2 (example shown over Scarborough carrying Sidewinder and Sparrow air-to-air missiles and BL755 bombs) ground attack and reconnaissance version entered service in No 6 Sqn from 7th May 1969, and in its FG1 defence interceptor role from 1st September that year in No 43 Sqn.

A naval aircraft originally, the Hawker Siddeley (formerly Blackburn) Buccaneer S2 entered RAF service ex-Royal Navy from 12th September 1969, supplemented by forty-three built for the RAF in the strike role. The Buccaneer can carry 1000-lb bombs or rockets, or Martel air-to-surface missiles.

**Harrier and Jaguar**  Developed from the Kestrel FGA1, the world's first vertical-take-off and strike fighter, which equipped a Tripartite Squadron of UK, USA and Federal German pilots at RAF West Raynham in October 1964, the Harrier entered RAF service with No 1 Sqn at Wittering in July 1969. Initially seventy-seven Harrier GR1 single-seat VTOL fighters and thirteen two-seat T2s operational trainers were built for the RAF. In May 1969 a Harrier, refuelled over the Atlantic by Victors, made the crossing in 6 hours 11 minutes to win the *Daily Mail* Transatlantic Air Race. In March 1970 nine Harriers of No 1 Sqn made their first overseas deployment to Akrotiri, Cyprus, and in the mid-1970s three Harrier squadrons were deployed in RAF Germany. A Harrier of No 20 Sqn is seen rising from a forest hide.

The Anglo-French Jaguar tactical support lightweight fighter of high performance, like the Harrier, was produced in GR1 single-seat and T2 two-seat versions. The first service Jaguar was delivered to RAF Lossiemouth on 30th May 1973 and, in the mid-'seventies, took over as the standard RAF ground attack fighter, releasing Phantoms for the air defence role to supplement and replace the ageing Lightnings. Plans are for eight RAF squadrons of Jaguars to be allotted to NATO.

**"The Red Arrows"**   The Royal Air Force Aerobatic Team, "the Red Arrows", was first formed in 1965 with six Gnat T1s, increased to nine the following year. Their livery has altered in successive years but the aircraft are essentially red. They have exhibited their immaculate flying on the Continent, in the Middle East and in America; altogether, they have given over a thousand performances. Pilots normally serve for three years with the team which comprises nine pilots, a manager, adjutant and engineer officer, twenty-eight airmen crew and ten Gnat T1 two-seat trainers.

In the 'fifties and 'sixties the RAF aerobatic team were represented by squadrons using first-line aircraft, Meteors, Hunters and Lightnings, but since the mid-'sixties, the service aerobatic teams have been training aircraft. Aerobatics are a normal part of pilot training syllabus to give confidence in ability and in the aircraft, and so carrying out to some degree of concept of flying training as practised in 1918. A new trainer, the Hawker Siddeley Hawk, came into service in 1977.

**"The Bulldogs" and "The Gazelles"** Taking over from the
Chipmunk trainers of the "Blue Chips" in 1974, "The Bulldogs" from
No 3 Flying Training School, Leeming, are the only RAF display-team
operating piston-engined aircraft. They are seen here over Durham
Cathedral. The Scottish Aviation Bulldog (originally a Beagle design)
replaced the Chipmunk as a primary trainer in the mid-'seventies.

Following the delivery of a small batch of Gazelle HT3s to the helicopter
branch of the Central Flying School in July 1973, a helicopter display-
team was formed the following year with school instructors.

**"The Pelicans"** For twenty years the Central Flying School has maintained an aerobatic team of Jet Provosts, starting with four T1s for the 1957 and 1958 seasons as "The Sparrows". Narrowed to an exhibition duet by "The Redskins", Flt Lts P. J. Hirst and J. R. Rhind, in 1959, the team was reconstituted in 1960 with four T3s, and two years later with five T4s when the name "Red Pelicans" was first used (the name coming from the School's badge). They are seen left with their T4s in 1963. For the 1970 season it was T5s in the then new Training Command livery of white, signal red and grey.

**"The Poachers"**    From the Royal Air Force College, Cranwell, come "The Poachers", formed in 1969, seen here over their home ground flying Jet Provost T4s which were replaced by T5s in the 'seventies. All pilots are qualified flying instructors who carry out display flying additional to their normal duties.

239

**Maritime Reconnaissance**   Derived from the Lincoln, an enlarged Lancaster, the Shackleton served from February 1951 when the MR1 entered service at Kinloss. After fifty-nine had been delivered, the MR2 supplemented those in service, but such were the differences that in 1954, under a general "swap-round", Nos 120, 206, 220, 240 and 269 Sqns had MR1s and Nos 37, 38, 42, 204, 224 and 228 Sqns had MR2s. The MR3 final production version featured a nosewheel and introduced tiptanks raising fuel capacity to 4,248 gallons. The last MR3 was delivered mid-1959, but throughout the 'sixties improvements were incorporated. A Shackleton MR3 of No 120 Sqn is shown above. Some of the early Mk 1s were made to T4 standard for operational training but the majority were replaced by Nimrods in the early 'seventies. There was an exception: to meet a requirement for an interim early-warning airborne station, twelve MR2s were converted to AEW2s, entering service at Kinloss with No 8 Sqn in January 1972. The Nimrod, based on the design of the Comet and the world's first jet maritime reconnaissance aircraft, entered service in October 1969 with the Maritime Operational Conversion Unit at St Mawgan. The example below is of No 42 Sqn.

## The RAF Mid-70s

| Aircraft/Missile | Command Deployment and Squadrons |
|---|---|
| Vulcan B2 | Strike Nos 9, 35, 44, 50, 101, 617 |
| Vulcan SR1 | Strike No 27 |
| Buccaneer S2 | Strike Nos 12, 208, RAF Germany Nos 15, 16 |
| Jaguar GR1 | RAF Germany Nos 14, 17, 31. Strike Nos 6, 54 |
| Harrier GR1/3 | RAF Germany Nos 3, 4, 20, Strike No 1 |
| Lightning F2/3/6 | RAF Germany Nos 19, 92. Strike Nos 5, 11 |
| Phantom FG1/ FGR2 | Strike Nos 23, 29, 41, 43, 56, 111, RAF Germany No 2 |
| Canberra PR7/9 | Malta No 13, Strike No 39 (for photo recce) |
| Canberra B2/T17 | Nos 7, 100 (target facilities), No 360 (counter-measures) |
| Nimrod MR1 | Strike (No 18 Group) Nos 42, 120, 201, 206, Malta No 203 |
| Victor K1/2 | Strike Nos 55, 57, 214 (tanker force) |
| Shackleton AEW2 | Strike No 8 (for airborne early warning) |
| Belfast C1 | Strike No 53 (later disbanded) |
| VC10 C1 | Strike No 10 (long-range transport) |
| Hercules C1 | Strike Nos 24, 30, 47, 70 (tactical transports) |
| Hunter FGA9 | Strike Nos 45, 58 (ground attack) |
| Wessex HC2 | RAF Germany No 18, Strike No 72, Hong Kong No 28 |
| Puma HC1 | Strike Nos 33, 230 (Wessex support helicopters) |
| Whirlwind HAR10 | Strike Nos 22, 202, No 84 Cyprus (Search and Rescue) |
| Bloodhound | Strike No 85, RAF Germany No 25 (anti-aircraft defence missiles) |
| Rapier | RAF Germany and Strike, RAF Regiment manned |
| Tornado GR1 & F2 on order | |

Most of the above units were NATO-assigned. In addition there were No 32 (Andover, HS125, Whirlwind), No 60 (Andover, Devon, Pembroke) and No 207 (Devon, Pembroke) communications squadrons, No 51 Sqn for radar calibration. Operational Conversion Units were: Nos 226 (Jaguar), 228 (Phantom), 230 (Vulcan), 231 (Canberra), 232 (Victor), 233 (Harrier), 235 (Nimrod), 237 (Buccaneer), 241 (VC10 and Belfast), 242 (Hercules).

(Units and figures based on tabulation by Air Pictorial, 1976).

**Regiment – Projectiles to Missiles** The Bofors gun (above) was used by the RAF Regiment in Germany, the Near, Middle and Far East, from World War II until the mid-'seventies. In 1970 the Short Tigercat short-range surface-to-air missile was introduced, followed in 1974 by the British Aircraft Corporation's Rapier low-level air defence missile system seen below with an operator acquiring a target to which the missiles on the launcher, left, can be automatically guided and commanded to follow the operator's line of sight to the target. The Rapier missiles are simple, supersonic and direct-hitting and have been deployed in RAF Germany.

HIGHLAND AREA
RADAR

SCOTTISH AIR TRAFFIC
CONTROL

BORDER AREA
RADAR

ULSTER AREA
RADAR

REMOTE
RADAR SITE

NORTHERN
AREA RADAR

REMOTE
RADAR SITE

MIDLAND
AREA RADAR

EASTERN
AREA
RADAR

COTSWOLD AREA
RADAR

LONDON AIR
TRAFFIC CONTROL

REMOTE
RADAR
SITE

REMOTE
RADAR-SITE

REMOTE
RADAR
SITE

## MATO UNIT LOCATIONS

**Military Air Traffic Organization (MATO)**    The RAF is vitally
concerned with Air Traffic Control both within and by integration with
the UK National Air Traffic Control Services. Within this organization,
MATO, operated by the RAF, supervises and controls military air
traffic, other than at Service airfields, through regional centres as
mapped. The RAF Ensign flew at London Airport in the 'sixties when the
London Centre was housed in temporary buildings at Heathrow, but this
eighty-strong RAF unit moved to the new London Air Traffic Control
Centre at West Drayton in 1971. Controllers are trained at the Joint Air
Traffic Control Area Radar School Sopley where, by the end of 1969, the
thousandth controller passed through training.

**Way Out West** A final act of Empire. While British Honduras (Belize) was being groomed for independence, there was increased military activity near the border with Guatemala during November 1974. Charged with responsibility to maintain the defence of the colony, it was reinforced in November 1975 by a detachment of Harriers flight-refuelled over the Atlantic by Victor tankers. Two are seen above over the Cays, a group of islands off Belize, and below Ferret 4 armoured cars of the 1st Battalion The Devonshire and Dorset Regiment are seen after being flown in by an RAF Belfast (below, left). Britannias and Hercules were also involved in the airlift and the maintenance of the reinforcements. However, under defence economies, ten Belfasts, the RAF's heavy freighters, were withdrawn in 1976, and the single squadron (No 53 Sqn) operating them was disbanded.

**North and South — Rigs and Gib**  A new task for the RAF, oil rig protection and patrol, epitomized above by a Vulcan from Scampton flying near a North Sea rig in August 1976. Gibraltar remains as much an RAF responsibility as ever. Although an international airport, flying control is provided by the RAF who handle some 7,500 movements annually. The station has NATO defence responsibilities and, as part of Strike Command, can be reinforced in a matter of hours. Below, Buccaneers of No 12 Sqn (note fox-head badge in deference to their earlier equipment) are seen in 1976 during the NATO maritime exercise "Open Gate". Another RAF aspect of Gibraltar is the radar and wireless stations and some of the hundred or so masts can be seen in this view.

**Nostalgia in the 'Seventies**    The Battle of Britain Memorial Flight, formed at Biggin Hill in 1957, moved successively to Martlesham Heath and Boscombe Down and was based at Coltishall from 1964 until 1st March 1976, when it moved to Coningsby. During the mid-'seventies the Flight consisted of two Hurricanes, LF363 (shown) and PZ865 the last built, and four Spitfires: Mk II P7350, Mk V AB910 and Mk XIXs PM631 (shown) and PS853, plus the Lancaster PA474 shown opposite. Pilots of the flight are volunteers, and the aircraft are in demand at some hundred shows each year; but due to their age – the oldest dates back to 1940 – severe limitations have to be placed on their use, and the Flight usually operate as a Hurricane/Spitfire pair, as shown, for flying exhibition purposes.

The RAF Museum, seen below shortly before completion, was opened by HM the Queen on 15th November 1972 and to the public two days later. Built on the site of RAF Hendon and incorporating one of the original hangars in the structure, it was established to preserve and display aviation exhibits and material of historic interest to the RAF and the nation. The collections housed include aircraft, personal relics, trophies and awards and uniforms covering all aspects of RAF life. While the running costs of the Museum are met from public funds, the initial cost was met by the Museum Trustees from public appeal; admission is free. An extension, the Dermot Boyle Wing for temporary exhibitions, was opened in 1976. Museum Director from its inception is Dr John Tanner and the Deputy Director J. M. Bruce.

Vintage Pair – a display pair formed in 1972 with Vampire T11 XH304 and Meteor WA669; the latter replaced later by WF791 shown. They are seen over Little Rissington, where the Central Flying School re-formed postwar on 7th May 1946 and which was handed over to the Army in 1976 when the pair moved to Cranwell. Apart from the veteran aircraft flying and the static display of some forty aircraft in the RAF Museum, there are displays at RAF Cosford Aerospace Museum and RAF St Athan which has British, German and Japanese aircraft; both these stations have taken over aircraft from the former museum at Colerne closed in 1976. Also, at a number of RAF stations, are historic aircraft as "gate guardians".

The only flying Lancaster maintained by the RAF, Mk I PA474, seen in 1976 flying over Trafalgar Square where a Lancaster was once displayed for a wartime "Wings for Victory" week.

**Goodbye to Gan** A wartime staging post was made at Gan in Addu Atoll, the southernmost of the Maldive Islands. In 1956 the Maldavian Government agreed to the re-activation of the airfield and in 1960 to a further airfield at Hulele some three hundred miles distant, which was later abandoned. During the 'sixties Gan became an important staging route for reinforcing Singapore and Malaya under South-East Asia Treaty Organization (SEATO) obligations. With revised defence policies, Gan was handed over to the Republic of the Maldives on 29th March 1976. Pictures show the last take-off from Gan as an RAF airfield by a Belfast conveying the run-down party, 29th March 1976, following the lowering of the RAF standard on the island, seen left.

**New Finishes and Weapons** For their sixteen years of service in the UK, the Lightnings had been in natural metal finish, but camouflaged finish in brown and green was introduced, and the Lightning F6s of No 5 Sqn at Binbrook are seen during the transitional period in March 1976. For aircraft operating in the ground attack role, a new weapon was introduced in 1975, the British-designed BL755 Cluster bomb which each eject over a hundred bomblets to saturate an area, seen here carried externally on the wing pylons of a Phantom FGR2 of 41 Sqn, Coningsby.

**Clubs and Associations**   The Royal Air Force Club resulted from generous gifts totalling £350,000 by Lord Cowdray, a former President of the Air Board, who did much to foster the creation of an Air Ministry. His intention was to create a memorial to his son, killed on the Western Front, and pay tribute to the "brilliant and superlatively heroic work" of the air arms in World War I. The closure of the former Royal Flying Corps Club in Bruton Street at the end of 1918, on the expiration of an endowment by Major Bersey, gave the new RAF Club its first premises, and in January 1922 the present magnificent premises in Piccadilly shown, overlooking Green Park, were opened. Membership is currently over nineteen thousand officers and ex-officers of the RAF, WRAF and PMRAFNS, Commonwealth and foreign air Forces; details from the Secretary, 128, Piccadilly, London W1. Telephone: 01–499–3456.

The Royal Air Forces Association (RAFA), founded during World War I, acquired its present title in 1943 and was granted a Royal Charter in 1952. Membership, currently in excess of 106,255, is open to all who served or are serving in the Royal Air Force and Women's Royal Air Force, as well as the antecedent arms, RAF Reserve and Volunteer Reserve, Royal Auxiliary Air Force, Princess Mary's RAF Nursing Service and of Air Forces of the Colonies and Dependencies and of nations that are members of the Commonwealth. Application for membership may be made to RAFA Central Headquarters, 43 Grove Park Road, London W4 3RU. Telephone 01–994–8504.

The Association in 1975 collected £340,808 through its Wings Appeal for its welfare and advisory services and Homes.

The Association has been forging closer ties with the serving RAF, and to commemorate the first fifty years of powered flight the Association annually presents their Wright Jubilee Trophy to the winner of an aerobatic competition among flying instructors of the RAF.

The Royal Air Force Benevolent Fund was founded by Viscount Trenchard on 23rd October 1919 to secure lasting benefits for the personnel of the flying services and their dependants in commemoration of their achievements in World War I. The Fund exists for the relief of distress or need, actual or potential, among past and serving members of the RAF, RAuxAF, WRAF and RAF Reserves and their dependants. Those wishing to contribute to the Fund or who are seeking assistance should write to the RAF Benevolent Fund, 67 Portland Place, London W1N 4AR.

The RAF Memorial standing on Victoria Embankment, London, overlooking the Thames, was erected through the offices of the Fund in memory of the officers and men of the flying services who died in World War I. It was unveiled by the Prince of Wales in July 1923. An inscription in remembrance of those men and women of the Air Forces of the British Commonwealth and Empire who gave their lives in World War II was unveiled by Viscount Trenchard on 15th September 1946. Additionally the Fund provided a home and school for the sons of deceased airmen established in 1921 at Vanbrugh Castle, Blackheath, London, for forty-two lads, increased to seventy in 1939 with gifts received. In 1976 the school moved to near Ewhurst, Surrey to merge with Woolpit School, and daughters as well as sons may be admitted in future.

The Pathfinder Association and Club originated in Pathfinder Force of Bomber Command formed on 15th August 1942 and re-designated No 8 (Pathfinder) Group on 8th January 1943, commanded by Air Vice-Marshal D. C. T. Bennett during its operational period. The Pathfinder Club was founded by the Pathfinder Association in 1944, and membership is open to all serving and former members of the RAF, Commonwealth and Allied Air Forces, for a modest subscription and initial entrance fee, the latter waived for ex-Pathfinders. For Association Membership, which automatically makes them members of the club, details are available from The Secretary, Pathfinder Association Ltd, 49 Grosvenor Street, London W1.

251

**The Royal Family and the Royal Air Force**    Her Majesty the Queen, Air Commodore-in-Chief of the Royal Air Force Regiment, Royal Auxiliary Air Force and Royal Observer Corps, and Commandant-in-Chief of the Royal Air Force College, Cranwell, is seen here on a visit to an RAF station. Her Majesty Queen Elizabeth The Queen Mother, Commandant-in-Chief of the Women's Royal Air Force, is seen here talking to ex-members of the Force.

Marshal of the Royal Air Force His Royal Highness Prince Philip, Duke of Edinburgh, KG PC KT OM GBE, who is Air Commodore-in-Chief of the Air Training Corps and a Marshal of the Royal Australian Air Force, is seen at the controls of a Wessex helicopter.

Left to right: Air Marshal Her Royal Highness Princess Alice, Duchess of Gloucester, GCB, CI GCVO, GBE, Air Chief Commandant of the Women's Royal Air Force; Her Royal Highness Princess Alexandra, GCVO, Air Chief Commandant of Princess Mary's Royal Air Force Nursing Service, and His Royal Highness Prince Charles, who trained as a pilot in the RAF holds the rank of Wing Commander.

# Index